THEOLOGY AS A SURPRISE

Theology
As a Surprise

Patristic and Pastoral Insights

Maxim Vasiljević

Bishop of the Western American Diocese of the
Serbian Orthodox Church in North and South America

ST VLADIMIR'S SEMINARY PRESS
YONKERS, NY 10707
2018

Library of Congress Cataloging-in-Publication Data

Names: Vasiljević, Maksim, 1968– author. | Behr, John, author of introduction.
Title: Theology as a surprise : Patristic and pastoral insights / Maxim Vasiljevic.
Description: Yonkers, NY : St. Vladimirs Seminary Press, 2018. | Includes
    bibliographical references.
Identifiers: LCCN 2018030020 (print) | LCCN 2018032261 (ebook) | ISBN
    9780881416275 | ISBN 9780881416268 (alk. paper)
Subjects: LCSH: Theology. | Orthodox Eastern Church—Doctrines. | Fathers of the
    Church.
Classification: LCC BX320.3 (ebook) | LCC BX320.3 .V372 2018 (print) | DDC
    230/.19—dc23
LC record available at https://lccn.loc.gov/2018030020

COPYRIGHT © 2018

ST VLADIMIR'S SEMINARY PRESS

575 Scarsdale Rd, Yonkers, NY 10707

1–800–204–2665

www.svspress.com

ISBN 978–0–88141–626–8 (paper)
ISBN 978–0–88141–627–5 (electronic)

Contents

Foreword

FR JOHN BEHR

IN THIS BOOK, His Grace Bishop Maxim (Vasiljević) offers us a breath of fresh air. This is not a book of theology in the form we have become accustomed to expect: a systematic examination of the usual topics of theological reflection; it is much more than that. Bishop Maxim draws upon Scripture, the Fathers, and Liturgy to address perennial and yet very contemporary questions: our experience of time and history, our existence as human persons and the complexities of sexuality and gender, our life in the *polis* and the *ekklēsia*, and the relational presence of an icon in a world saturated with digital images. And he does so in engagement with a diverse range of contemporary thinkers: philosophers, scientists, poets, artists, media figures, and film directors—indeed, almost every chapter begins with a line from a movie. Not, perhaps, what one might have expected from a bishop but, then again, perhaps our expectations need to be raised!

The theological vision and call that emerges here is indeed a surprise, and one that brings the gospel to bear on all aspects of our life and existence. One theme that runs as a guiding thread throughout the essays in this work is the theological commitment to seeing and understanding all things from the perspective of the eschaton, anticipated proleptically (and not simply "realized") in the Eucharist, where we are drawn together, and therefore relationally, into the one Body of the risen Christ. This eschatological and eucharistic emphasis, centered upon the person in relation, is one that His Grace learned well from his teacher, His Eminence Metropolitan John (Zizioulas); but it is carried through with an original, sure, and clear voice—one that is very much Bishop Maxim's own. This eschatological dimension is not simply, as it so often is, a matter of "the last things," treated last by systematic theology (after expounding the doctrine of God, creation, salvation, and so on); it is, rather, the *starting point* for theology. In the end, to paraphrase T. S. Eliot, we have our beginning. As Bishop Maxim forcefully points out in the opening essays, it is the future that determines the past. Hence the title of this work: theology is a *surprise*. Truth is not found in that which is self-evident, for that which appears to be self-evident now, in the present, is not in reality so; the truth of the present (and the past) has yet to be determined by the future, which is, however, already given in the person of Christ himself, crucified and risen; he is the end to which all things tend, for all things end in death, but a death that is now, through the cross, the entrance to life.

This means, as Bishop Maxim points out when explaining the title of the work in the introduction, that theology is never simply about the self-evident, nor merely a preservation or repetition of that which we (wrongly) assume to be so. This is so for two reasons. First, everything must be verified by the future, not the past; and so, as he puts it, "in the rise of every new epoch, things of the past ought to be restated and rephrased." Second, just as the events of salvation were only understood in retrospect, "so true Christians question themselves continually, instinctively, and subject their judgments and engagements to the testing scrutiny of an intervening awareness of assurance rooted in their relation to the Holy Spirit, who *suddenly* brings the 'last things' into history." The Orthodox Christian Tradition is never merely repetition or preservation, but, as His Eminence Metropolitan Kallistos

(Ware) put it, a "faithful creativity." This places us in a position that is at the same time both one of great responsibility and also one of the greatest freedom, a freedom that does not know the fear that too often drives us to retreat into the past. It is with this responsible freedom that Bishop Maxim tackles, with great creativity, issues that address us today and will continue to do so, with ever greater complexity, in the foreseeable future.

According to Kierkegaard, we only ever understand backwards, but we must live forwards. Bishop Maxim, having spent years immersed in the works of the Fathers, especially St Maximus the Confessor, has already been formed in the mind of the Fathers. In the present work, this "understanding backwards" is treated with a light touch, for the emphasis here is on living and thinking forwards, facing the contemporary world and its questions by drawing new theological treasures—often surprising and always insightful—out of the old.

INTRODUCTION

Against the Self-Evident

For in the realm of truth, repetition is surprise.
— Elder Vasileios of Iveron[1]

THIS BOOK IS AN ATTEMPT to express the principle (*logos*, reason) and the mode (*tropos*, way) of the things we experience through various reflections on important concepts such as time, death, art, gender, icons, mercy, law, council, and so on. The title of the book implies that we reject the notion of self-explanatory truths. There are two reasons for that. First, everything in this world must be verified by the future: in the rise of every new epoch, things of the past ought to be restated and rephrased. Second, the events of salvation are more clear in retrospect than they were in prospect. So true Christians question themselves continually, instinctively, and subject their judgments and engagements to the testing scrutiny of an intervening awareness of assurance rooted in their relation to the Holy Spirit, who *suddenly*[2] brings the "last things" into history.

We cautiously use the word "surprise" (astonishment) instead of using the word "excitement," which has in our time generally become synonymous with "adrenaline rush." We know that human desires use various forms of disguise; they arouse a sensory excitement and seek

[1]Elder Vasileios of Iveron, *"The Light of Christ Shines upon All" Through All the Saints*, trans. Elizabeth Theokritoff (Montreal, Quebec: Alexander Press, 2001), 12.

[2]Cf. Acts 2.2. All New Testament quotations are from the RSV, unless otherwise noted.

quick satiation. By optimizing the demand for fame and favorability, the postmodern superego surprises us by "sanctifying" pleasure. As opposed to this, here we speak about the God of the Bible, who surprises man and history in an apocalyptic way, so that they exclaim, "*Whence [is] this to me?*"[3] Hence, the readier we are to receive them, the more surprising, perplexing, and dramatic are the revelations that follow.

Perhaps one might find it too far-fetched for a theologian to dialogue not only with the Cappadocian Fathers, St Maximus the Confessor, Georges Florovsky, and Anthony Bloom, but also with Yuval Noah Harari, Van Gogh, Steve Jobs, Stella Adler, Andrei Tarkovsky, Brian Greene, Bill Maher, and Dustin Hoffman, to mention a few. However, I believe that we can be informed by such a dialogue, since we all express the same hope and the pain of the same humanity. St Maximus the Confessor once said, "For it is good to draw on examples from our own life to point to the truth of the realities that are above us."[4] It is with this striking advice in mind that we begin to pursue our inquiry.

The four parts of this book are critical to this argument, but they can be read individually. Our belief is that the distinctly *ecclesial* point of view is not a matter of simply and solely drawing from particular sources. When the truth is presented to the rest of the world in an accessible and compelling way, then a new impulse inspires a real expanding of the horizon. Indeed, in the Church there are so many approaches, but, luckily, there is no Babel. Although this mixture of sources looks like a pretty broad brush, it is hard to neglect the striking phrase (repeated six times in the plural) in the Synodikon of Orthodoxy (843): "According to the divinely inspired *theologies* (θεολογίας) of the saints."[5]

[3]Lk 1.43.

[4]*Amb.* 32.

[5]See Jean Gouillard, "Le Synodikon de l'orthodoxie: Édition et commentaire," *Travaux et Mémoires* 2 (1967): 83.

* * *

Part I deals with time, death, and resurrection. Long before Gadamer, St Paul introduced the *future* as a hermeneutical tool for historical events, saying that "if the dead are not raised, then Christ has not been raised."[6] The reasoning behind Paul's conclusion is so subtle that even today it takes a lot of logical effort to appreciate it fully. The "pre-happening" of the future of the world in Christ's Resurrection speaks of the future's work in progress within our feeble human condition. This idea is strongly suggested by a number of well-reasoned considerations. The future has such an ontological significance that it acquires "substance."[7] It is only when the Son of Man is lifted up that we will know that *he is*.[8] Also, the future can be "anticipated," thus becoming part of our memory. This makes it possible for one to talk about *remembrance of the future*, and this precisely is what happens in the divine Eucharist. These are some of the most prominent ideas discussed in Part I of this book, emphasizing the Resurrection as an event that defies explanation. Debate on the issues discussed in this chapter will no doubt continue as we grope to understand what time, death, and resurrection actually are. With the development of eschatology (as a proleptic ontology that begins with the future and works backward to the present), the tension only intensifies.

* * *

"What if your desires unlocked hidden secrets?" This is a profound psychological question of the twentieth century. *Who knows what might fly out of anybody's mouth at any moment?* When Bill Maher recently overstepped his privilege as a comedian, it was merely a symptom of

[6]1 Cor 15.16.
[7]Cf. Heb 11.1.
[8]Cf. Jn 8.28.

the unexpected in human psychology.[9] Modern science is attempting to understand human freedom mostly as a genetically determined neurochemical process. The scientific world view has influenced modern man in his desire to discover a basic hormonal predisposition for taste, fashion, political choices, concerns, preoccupations, and, finally, religiosity. As we will see later in this book, key developments in modern biology have established the existence of various forms of hormone-driven behavior,[10] none of which set an absolute standard for man's freedom, but all of which thoroughly challenge the naïve conception of what it means for humans to be free. In such a scenario, how can one be holy and unique? So, maybe it is time to examine genes and hormones in light of the anthropological experience of the Church, especially in association with its basic idea of *freedom*. Do any other plausible instances of freedom exist in the basic biochemistry of the human raw materials required for living processes, which drive us toward holiness and uniqueness? Does gender have a future? Part II in this volume will take up these questions.

* * *

It seems that contemporary theology is the guardian of the sanctity of man's personhood. We deal with this in Part III, which bears the title "Mercy, Law, and Council." By taking sinners into the community of the eschatological meal with himself, Jesus introduced another ethos

[9]Bill Maher transgressed his privilege as a comedian when he made an inexcusable remark using the n-word. Wesley Morris, "What Was Bill Maher's Big Mistake?," *New York Times*, June 4, 2017, https://www.nytimes.com/2017/06/04/arts/television/what-was-bill-mahers-big-mistake.html.

[10]There is an interaction between hormones and behavior. As chemical messengers released from the endocrine glands, hormones influence the nervous system to regulate behaviors such as aggression, mating, and parenting of individuals. Yet, the freedom we are talking about here is not a neurological capacity, but relates to the acceptance or refusal of our own being, of the world, and of God himself.

and logic: he came as a stranger and surprised his own people (previously, he had come to *his own* people, and they did not receive him). Some Christian charitable endeavors have sown confusion and led to misunderstandings. On the one hand, the Church should do its charitable social activity (or any ethical or political act), but with awareness and criteria drawn from the theology. Namely, if we endanger our basic, ultimate principles in order to apply them, then we are engaged in a sociology detached from ecclesiology (i.e., mimicking other social programs). On the other hand, caring solely about eschatology while giving the cold shoulder to those in need is not the position of the Church. As of today, the question of the exact *measure of social involvement* of the Church does not have a unique, definite answer. The Holy and Great Council in Crete of 2016 stressed that the Orthodox understanding of man is opposed both to the arrogant apotheosis of individual rights and to "the humiliating debasement of the human person within the vast contemporary structures of economy, society, politics, and communication."[11] Our right to become gods (the right of deification), as a right of personhood, seems to be neglected in the human rights debate. The new conciliar/synodal era enables us to take concrete steps to increase the voice of the local churches in the witness and governance of the universal Church. Can councils serve as a corrective for modern democracy? The ancient Church transformed synodality from a political phenomenon into a theological one. The Church goes beyond the political meaning that we observe in the ancient Hellenes and Romans (the forum, elected representatives, the republic, decision-making in the senate, etc.), and it links the notion of "synod" to eucharistic judgment—something that eventually leads the Holy Fathers to link the term "synod" to Christ himself or the Holy

[11]"Encyclical of the Holy and Great Council of the Orthodox Church," *Annual 2016 of the Western American Diocese* (Los Angeles: Sebastian Press 2016), 38.

Trinity—that is, to theology. A Church that acts in a conciliar/synodal way has to do with man, and not with an ideological movement.

* * *

Is there truth in art? Do any plausible instances of truthfulness in art exist in the fabric of human creativity, including digital iconicity? Part IV in this volume will take up this question. "When a work exceeds the meaning it initially seems to convey, that is because there is a *poetic* element in it."[12] Taking into account some assessments from the history of art, we deduce that truth in art does not simply correspond to the mind or reality. A definition of truth must point to the "relationality" or referentiality of the common ground of existence that we share (truth in existential terms). The iconic approach of the Church presupposes that one accepts the existence of a presence to which one can relate. But the real challenge is this: how do we cope with the turbulence caused by new technology? Here we discuss the icon and digital iconicity. This section is also concerned with the question of how to survive in the age of automation. Our culture so badly needs "information asceticism" and "digital apophatism," by which we mean abstinence from giving the ultimate priority to virtual reality.

* * *

In the new world, the Church must play a leading part in dialoguing with the prevailing culture at the deepest level. In the patristic period, the fact that the Church entered into a deep dialogue with the culture prevented others from stepping in and taking over. The "Jews of the Diaspora" (the so-called "Hellenizers") in the second and third centuries paved the way for the then "*oikoumenē*" (the Greek and Roman world) to accept the Word Incarnate; they played a definitive part

---

[12]Roland Barthes, *Signs and Images* (London: Seagull Books, 2016), 145.

in clarifying the Christian faith and giving it shape. In like manner, the "Orthodox of the Diaspora" are the only reliable link with today's *oikoumenē*. The path opened up by the early Hellenizers was not one that would ever close again. It was the path followed by St Peter, with the vision that spurred him to baptize Gentiles, which he did without making circumcision a condition of baptism. This path was also followed by a second great hellenizing Jew, St Paul, who would shape the whole history of Christianity by preaching the acceptance of Gentiles into the Church.

The Orthodox churches in the USA should use Paul's genius and grace for mission to open unexpected avenues for dialogue between Orthodoxy and the many other kinds of Christians in the increasingly pluralistic world of our time. This can reopen that historic route of Christianity, making Orthodoxy a relevant world Church and allowing it to avoid marginalization. In this task, we pray that the ultimate love of Christ causes a divine perplexity and peaceful surprise which will remain forever within his Church.

I should like to express my warmest thanks to Sally Anne Boyle for her invaluable assistance in editing this book. My thanks are also due to Jasmina Boulanger, Fr Vasileios Thermos, Fr Gregory Edwards, and Dionysios Skliris for reading the manuscript.

I would also like to express my thanks to Fr John Behr, a precious friend and Professor of Patristics, St Vladimir's Seminary, New York, for his kindness in writing a foreword to this book.

PART I

Time, Death, and Resurrection

The Beginning and the End Are Not the Same

TIME IN ECCLESIAL LIFE

> Here's the thing about the future. Every time you look
> at it, it changes—because you looked at it—and that
> changes everything else.
> —Cris Johnson, *Next*, directed by Lee Tamahori

IN HIS POPULAR BOOK, *The Fabric of the Cosmos: Space, Time, and the Texture of Reality*, American theoretical physicist Brian Greene, after noting that "the past is not in any way altered by today's actions," poses a seemingly "theological" question: "If you can't change something that has already happened, can you do the next best thing and erase its impact on the present?"[1] Apart from being an intriguing question, this is also an example of cosmology actually coming close to being philosophy and even knocking at the door of theology.

Among the most common notions that humankind has ever confronted, time is one of the least understood. This topic is especially important in our time, in which today's lifestyle, fueled by technology, introduces another kind of chronotype, or concept of time, mainly due to the urges of modern "digital" life (and its symptoms: absence of

[1]Brian Greene, *The Fabric of the Cosmos: Space, Time, and the Texture of Reality* (New York: Vintage Books, 2005), 191.

patience, instant gratification, everything being supposed to happen *now*, etc.). Undoubtedly, time was always a very difficult dimension of life and memory for humans to master. Man's quest for a way to rise above the contrasts in time-reality leads him to realize that all these attempts are simply unsuccessful "digressions" from the irreversible flow of time, in which death mercilessly separates the past from the future and eliminates the "now" of time. From this difficulty stem all attempts to culturally construct temporal maps and images—aren't there many time registers, and thus many times?—in an effort to ease the practical difficulties of human life or, in some cases, to achieve a "diachronic" existence and enable an everlasting memory. From the Platonic escape from the momentary, the fleeting, and the ephemeral being, through the Proustian "search for lost time," we are led in our days, with the help of digital memory, to the extension of the mechanism of "panoptic control" into the past—since the Internet remembers what we want to be forgotten.

Why does time exist at all? What response can ecclesial theology offer to this deceptively simple question? The ecclesial answer, unavoidably suffused with various nuances, will frame our discussion in the pages that follow.

Our entire existence—everything we do, think, and experience—takes place during some interval of time. Time—according, it seems, to contemporary physics[2]—is a part of creation(hood), and every aspect of existence (language, thought, desire, etc.) is "chronic," time-bound. Space and time are fused together into what we call "space-time," *chōro-chronos*.[3] However, the ecclesial time of which we speak

---

[2]See, for example, Greene, *The Fabric of the Cosmos*.

[3]"Newton thought that motion through time was totally separate from motion through space—he thought these two kinds of motion had nothing to do with each other. But Einstein found that they are intimately linked." Greene, *The Fabric of the Cosmos*, 48.

is fundamentally different from the clock-time in which our quotidian rhythm of life operates. This is because the Church, by drawing the eschatological into time, offers "the assurance of things hoped for, the conviction of things not seen,"[4] so that time acquires an indispensable significance. God—who is not bound by the condition of time—obviously respects our time, as he knows that we need to go through expectancy,[5] that is, the unfolding of the future in time ("I *await* the resurrection of the dead"[6]). If historical time were simply enough—without the in-breaking of the future into the present—then what would be the significance of the Second Coming? But the New Testament presents a new vision of time, of *kairos*, which is an intervention of the Second Coming, "the last days"[7] into time, indicating that the future gives meaning and substance to the past. It is the *kairos*, that is, the *end*, that "justifies," that gives meaning to the past; all Christian hermeneutics depend on this *kairological* perspective.

The Problem of Time and History

Every approach to the question of time is faced with one initial question: Is it a real physical entity or simply a useful idea? In other words, how can one ascribe an essence to time, that is, to consider it as existing, if the givens constituting it—the past, the present, the future—are "non-existing"? They are inexistent because, at every moment, we are faced with the irretrievable past and with the distant or imminent future, thanks to death, which divides everything. None of these can

---

[4]Heb 11.1.

[5]Cf. Mk 4.26–28: "The kingdom of God is as if a man should scatter seed upon the ground, and should sleep and rise night and day, and the seed should sprout and grow, he knows not how. The earth produces of itself. . . ."

[6]Nicene-Constantinopolitan Creed.

[7]Acts 2.17.

be recognized as accessible in the present. According to Sartre, that which separates what is before and what is after is *nothingness*.[8] This is why, as the universal human experience throughout time confirms, time itself creates a serious problem for created beings, and particularly for humans.

This leads us to the postulate that the immanent goal of the entire flow of time is an unattainable future and that, in itself, time does not have a point of culmination or fulfillment. Yes, there is history, but it does not suffice without a future personal intervention that would unite the present, past, and future—not in a pretemporal divine event but in *history moving toward a hidden future*. With mythic time, the ancient Greeks presented the succession of time as a reality per se, which constantly changes the past into the present, being into non-being. (In this chronological awareness of time, the Greeks saw the mythical figure of the god Kronos/Saturn, who devoured his children.) Indeed, there is no finite progress within the infinitude of time, or, if I may borrow a phrase from St Justin (Popović) the New, there is only a "progress in the watermill of death."[9] The entire cycle of successive transformations in history *looks* preformulated and predetermined en route to a completed, seemingly "mature" state. But history does not necessarily conform to a certain plan, to the idea of efficient development. That would inevitably lead to a particular kind of logical "determinism" (fatalism). In his fallen state, man's obsession with himself and with things-themselves—immersed in time—blinds him to the things to come so that the *logos* of beings is not easily recognized.[10] So

[8]Jean-Paul Sartre, *Being and Nothingness: An Essay on Phenomenological Ontology* (London: Routledge Classics, 2003).

[9]Justin Popović, "The Progress in the Watermill of Death," in *Philosophical Crevasses* [in Serbian] (Ćelije Monastery, 1987), 28–50.

[10]There is an astounding dynamism hidden within human nature as its *logos*; yet, without a proper personal *tropos*, it is uncontrollable and purposeless.

whatever preestablished goal exists in the historical process, it is not attained and recognized automatically, and only the future event (a personal freedom and engagement) can discover its meaning.

Here we encounter one problem that everyone confronts in his or her experience. Where is this problem reflected, and what are the solutions to it? Allow me for a moment to turn to the response found in the history of philosophy.

This ambiguity in the human perception of time has led ancient philosophers to the conclusion that time is neither a given ontological reality in itself, nor a constitutive fact of the existing. A brief look at the seemingly simple concept of "now" can demonstrate this. Our human, experience-based perception accepts time as a succession or flow of moments, or units of time, where each of them, in order to be a unit, must be indivisible, and we call it "now." (We accept that "now" as non-quantifiable time.) However, we all live time as a fragmented sequence consisting of the past, present, and future (which could be seen as a series of snapshots, as Brian Greene suggests in his book *The Fabric of the Cosmos*). Aristotle reasonably demonstrated that the only real problem is the fact that at the present moment which we call the "present," there is nothing. In the Aristotelian sense, "now" (νῦν, moment) has no content, and, for Aristotle, it does not last, because it only unites the *proteron* and *hysteron* (priority and posteriority). The first consequence of this is that the past is able to acquire autonomy with regard to the future, to contain "facts" completely independent of the future. (Historians are preoccupied with this sort of history; they would like to have a sort of "chrono-zoom" on the timeline of all history, or a map of time.) So, givenness and choice are the two serious features and limitations of all created existences, both presupposing some kind of time, which is measured in seconds, minutes, hours, and years. However, time is not a universal tick-tock, because time does not tick the same for everyone (thus Kant made it a function of the individual subject), which makes unanswerable the question: Does time belong to beings or to nonbeings, and what is its nature? "Along the line of time there always remains 'just as much' ground to be covered before the goal is attained as there was today or yesterday."[11]

This real and experiential understanding of time easily leads us to view time as an objective cause of natural decay. However, all this happens only because of the reality of death, which our faith ascribes to the fall. The problem is not simply in a forward *flow* of time (because time has its downpours, rivers, setbacks, and overflows). The problem is death itself, which annihilates the *content* and *meaning* of this flow. Death eliminates from its being the "now" of time; so what exists now, because of death, is "past"—separated from the future. Therefore, "now" is just a mental border, a cut between the past and the future. Without something that is able to redeem it, time (sequential time) flows on without meaning, sunk in death, and nothing that happens within it survives. Everything in the space-time odyssey has chronological boundaries. Although nature's timing is impressive—the biological life cycle proceeds to its realization with a particularly expedient rhythm through internally substantiated stages—nothing can redeem particular beings from this vicious circle. Time is always on its own side (never on our side), and it has no regard for the person.

In that same sense, Elder Aimilianos rightly points out:

Human life is nothing more than a movement to, or away from, God. It is a journey, a progression, which God alone knows. For us, our life consists of traces left by the Holy Spirit, as He moves among us and breathes within us (cf. Rom 8.9–17; 2 Cor 6.16).

[11]Georges Florovsky, "The Metaphysical Premises of Utopianism," in *Philosophy: Philosophical Problems and Movements*, vol. 12 of *The Collected Works of Georges Florovsky* (Vaduz: Büchervertriebsanstalt, 1989), 84.

And when the Spirit comes and dwells within us, we arrive at the end of time, the limit of "now," which is a particle of time that in a sense is nonexistent, because as soon as you utter it, as soon as you become aware of it, it vanishes. And so we have arrived at the present moment, which has absolutely no meaning at all except *for as long as it is called "today"* (Heb 3.13), because who can say that he knows the limits of his life?

On the one hand, then, we have the "time" of man, which tends toward non-existence. On the other, we have the timeless time of God, which is His *walking about among us* (cf. 2 Cor 6.16; Lev 26.12); the touch of His Spirit in our lives, His active presence in our midst. But how can this timeless time become real for us? How can we arrive at that particular moment of time, which is not a limit, or a closure, but a revelation, an uncovering of the place where we stand with respect to God?[12]

Various Solutions to the Problem of Time

If the pathology of time, as we have seen, consists in the fact that "now" contains nothing, then different scenarios and possibilities arise to resolve the problem of time. Each scenario comes with profound implications for the concept of time.

a) *Prolonging the past and "expiration dates."* The first possibility is an attempt to prolong or expand the past as much as possible. This is what man tries to do with history and memory.[13] But this solution, as experience teaches us, has a very relative value: historical monuments of all kinds also have expiration dates, experience death, and sooner or later disappear or are forgotten.[14] However, this expiration or forgetting

---

[12]Archimandrite Aimilianos of Simonopetra, *The Way of the Spirit: Reflections on Life in God,* trans. Maximos Simonopetrites (Athens: Indiktos, 2009), 134.

[13]Cf. Herodotus.

[14]Cf. J. Zizioulas, "Eschatologie et société," *Irénikon* 73 (2000): 278–97.

is not a completely bad thing. Knowing expiration dates, especially in the digital era, reminds us of the temporary nature (and value) of most information; we, in fact, *need* to forget what is no longer needed.

b) *Flight from the present.* The second possibility is a complete escape from the present time. This, undoubtedly, can be done only on a psychological level, because, in reality, time continues to be fragmented, and we continue to suffer its consequences due to physical death. This perspective is offered by St Augustine, for whom time is, above all, an experience of the soul. Through remembering, the soul transfers the past and the future into an observing of the present. Throughout the works of St Augustine, there is a search for a universe that could rise above the unfortunate duality in time-reality to a unified system of worldwide peace and tranquility.[15]

c) *World of ideas.* The next possibility is a belief in something, such as the immortality of the soul or the world of ideas, that never dies ("time as a passing revelation and unclear copy of the eternity of the truly existing"[16]). Obviously, this is a Platonic rather than a biblical solution. Perhaps one aspect of this approach could be prayer, but only as an *ecstatic* effort (and not as a monologue) to overcome the gaps in time-reality. But how can one know when prayer is psychological self-satisfaction (making God the servant of man's desires), and when it is the real experience of a personal *relationship* with God? In Plato, time can be defined only with reference to the age, just as sensible beings are defined by their relationship with ideas. It is a relationship of analogy, between the image and the original.[17]

---

[15]"What is essential here is namely the ideal, universal, objective harmony of universal, cosmic existence. Grace is transformed into a natural force of this 'original,' objective sphere. Determinism is only one of the components of this universally organic world view." Florovsky, "Metaphysical Premises," 86.

[16]Plato, *Timaeus* 37b.5–7.

[17]See a different notion of "aeon" in St Maximus: "The aeon is time when it ceases

d) The past determines the future, and the utopian flux of history. Aristotle believed that time is related to the givenness of existence. He did not consider time as constitutive of being, but understood it as merely a number, that is, as a measure of motion and movement from the earlier to the later.[18] But the giveness of existence presupposes some kind of time since the "given" ontologically precedes the one to which it is "given."[19] The utopians accepted this Aristotelian concept and thus were obliged to conceive of and interpret history in teleological categories. According to this idea, historical time postpones or denies a "from-the-kingdom movement," which—as we will see later—runs against the forward current of progress.

e) Everlasting digital memory (and its dangers). This may seem to be a solution to the problem of time, but is (biological) forgetting a bad thing? If we look at it more carefully, we may actually find it to be a life-saving advantage. Incapable of forgetting, man remains forever caught in his memories and facts, which give shape to who he is. In *Delete*,[20] Viktor Mayer-Schönberger traces the important role that forgetting has played throughout human history, from the ability to make sound decisions unencumbered by the past, to the possibility of second chances. The written word made it possible for humans to remember across generations and time, yet now digital technology and

from movement, and time is the aeon when it is measured as carried forward by movement. So the aeon is time deprived of movement, time is the aeon measured by movement" (PG 91:1164BC).

[18]Time is the measure of movement, be it circular, sequential, or mixed. For the Fathers, the category of "when" is a universal category determining all created realities because of the universality of movement. Since it is possible to measure movement, therefore there is time (since time is the measure of movement).

[19]Aristotle, *Physics* IV.10–11, 218a30ff. In the case of God, nothing can be said to precede or be preceded.

[20]Viktor Mayer-Schönberger, *Delete: The Virtue of Forgetting in the Digital Age* (Princeton: Princeton University Press, 2009).

global networks are overriding our natural ability to forget—the past is irrevocably and ever present, ready to be called up at the click of a mouse and to oppress us as facts with their unquestionable authority.

f) Eucharist as incorrupt time. The Church has its own solution for created temporality, and it contains a complete and fully convincing answer to the question of time. In a nutshell, it allows a penetration into time, which abolishes the blind *continuity* of time (temporality as subjugation to the "before" and "after"), inserting into time not an interlude but the *duration* of the loving, "physical" communion between humanity and God. Liturgical time is a time of discontinuation from decay (at least in part), a "break" in the relentless arrow of time, and a liberty from the complete determination of past causes. It also suggests that time is essential to ecclesial life, an issue we will discuss later.

The Biblical-Patristic Response

From the beginning of ecclesial history, it was clear that, in the experience of the Church, time is of paramount importance: time is a part of creation. Time emerged at creation, making creation unimaginable without time. Since the Greek Fathers and St Augustine, this has been the common understanding, which has since been affirmed by modern physics. But the Bible offers a different and extremely significant perspective. Even a cursory study of the Bible reveals that there is a paradoxical structure in history, and particularly biblical history: (a) the future "precedes" the past; (b) everything that happens is not completed in the moment it happens, but acquires its meaning in the future; (c) one must *wait* if he or she wants to see what actually happened; (d) if the future does not come to show what actually happened, then it (the past event) has no meaning, that is, it does not exist. In this perspective, the future is more than just an aspect of time; in the

Bible, time is the future's work in progress, since God's promise or will (*thelēsis*) regulates the trajectory of history.

Let us take a closer look at this perspective and see how it relates to our topic.

a) *Time as a condition* sine qua non *of the being of all creatures.* Any denial of time leads to the denial of creation. For the Church, time is a blessing, an "affordance," and it is not necessary to escape from it,[21] since time and space are the conditions of God's presence in the world; it is an opportunity for things to happen, because history is a constant journey and tension between promise and fulfillment. Although temporal (and spatial) limitations are contravening predeterminations of existence and forms of the world's finitude, the Church's witness, received from the Jewish tradition, is that God created all things "very good," and evil cannot be inherent in God's creation.[22] When evil—which is basically the absence of love—is present, then time is shortened and space shrinks. However, time *itself* calls for a different temporality, for a sort of meta-time, which will redeem and judge it. This *new* temporality will put its stamp on historical persons and events by removing *evil*.

b) *Time needs redemption.* For this very reason, time needs judgment and redemption, and this can happen only with the victory over death, through the Cross ("now is the time for the judgment of this world"[23]) and the Resurrection. The Church did not acciden-

---

[21]"Space" and "time," in the Maximian system, seem to express "the intramundane action of God, what is called Providence." Cf. Pascal Mueller-Jourdan, "*Where* and *When* as Metaphysical Prerequisites for Creation in *Ambiguum* 10," in *Knowing the Purpose of Creation through the Power of the Resurrection*, ed. Maxim Vasiljević (Los Angeles: Sebastian Press, 2013), 295.

[22]Cf. Christos Yannaras, *The Enigma of Evil* (Brookline, MA: Holy Cross Orthodox Press, 2012).

[23]Jn 12.31.

tally put the Resurrection at the center of its life; the Resurrection is a victory over death and is identified with both the first (ἀπαρχὴ τῶν ἡμερῶν) and the eighth day,[24] and this victory wipes away all forms of evil. St Basil in his *Commentary on Hexameron* gives an interesting answer to the question, "Why is it said 'one' (μίαν) day, and not 'first' (πρώτην)?"[25] Because, he holds, this first day is an *icon* of the beginning of the age to come.[26] The logical consequence is compelling. If it were only the "first," it would be closed by the circle of seven, and then we would have to start again from the beginning. That is why it is said, "the day one," because it is the "eighth day" too, and the eighth day is outside the circle of seven (διὰ τὸ ἔξω κεῖσθαι τοῦ ἑβδοματικοῦ τούτου χρόνου),[27] since the eighth day is eschatological. In this way, closed circles of numbers are transcended, a manner that characterizes the entire Bible. For St Maximus the Confessor, the end is greater than the beginning: in the beginning, we have the state *kata physin*, while at the end there is a state *hyper physeōs*. For Origen, the end is a *copy* of the beginning ("the end is always like the beginning").[28] According to St Maximus, Pentecost falls on the fiftieth day because

[24]St Basil, *Commentary on Hexameron* (Thessaloniki: ΕΠΕ, 1973), 98.

[25]"And there was evening, and there was morning, the day one (ἡμέρα μία)" (Gen 1.5)

[26]μίαν ὠνόμασε τοῦ αἰῶνος τὴν εἰκόνα, τὴν ἀπαρχὴν τῶν ἡμερῶν (ibid.). Similarly, St Gregory the Theologian, in his *Oration* on Holy Pentecost, applies the same logic: "There was need of one day, *which we received from the age to come*, which was both the eighth day and the first day, or rather a single and perpetual day—for it is necessary that the Sabbath of souls celebrated here should reach its end there" (*Oration* 41.2 [SC 358:316–18, lines 33–36]).

[27]St Basil, *Commentary*, 98.

[28]Origen, *On First Principles* 1.6.2. Although Origen looks to the end in order to understand the beginning, he operates with the idea of "contemplation" or "reflection" and not of the "will" (*thelēsis*.) God does not simply *know* but He *wills* the end. The will involves freedom (self-determination) and drama (historical creativity), while contemplation, as in Evagrius, does not involve *history*. For Maximus, the end is greater than the beginning.

seven sevens is forty-nine, but the fiftieth day is a conclusion of the circle seven times seven, and its overcoming.[29] Therefore, Pentecost is the presence of the eschaton.

Contrary to what we might expect, at the Pascha, all are then invited to the feast of joy, "those who have fasted and those who have not fasted,"[30] those who came earlier and those who came at the eleventh hour. With this experiential and hermeneutical truth, the Church redeems time as well. Fr Georges Florovsky argues, "any 'objective' transfiguring of the cosmos without the Resurrection would not be an 'end.'"[31] The Resurrection of Christ has not happened unless we are resurrected,[32] so, *mutatis mutandis*, no event has existence unless it has been eschatologically confirmed. Hence, when the Church gathers at the eucharistic meal with the resurrected Christ, it serves, as St Ignatius of Antioch says, as the "medicine of immortality," an "antidote for death."[33] This language is biblical but also has to do with psychological experiences. There is a new concept of time hidden in this truth of the Eucharist—that it is both an "antidote for death" and an "authentic present," which does not abolish space-time.

c) *The time of Maranatha and the postponement of the Kingdom.* Now, we come to another important point. To fulfill time in history means to confront evil and the divisive powers that call for the postponement of the End. The demons ask Jesus, "Have you come here to

---

[29]"The eighth and the first, or rather, the one and perpetual day, is the unalloyed, all-shining presence of God, which comes about *after* things in motion have come to *rest*" (*Amb.* 65 [PG 91:1392CD]). For St Maximus, the freedom of the "deed," historical creativity, and agency ("motion") is crucial to his understanding of nature's *telos* ("rest").

[30] St John Chrysostom, *Catechetical Homily* (PG 59:721–24).

[31]Florovsky, "Utopianism," part V (missing in English edition, here quoted according to Serbian translation).

[32]Cf. 1 Cor 15.16.

[33]St Ignatius, *Letter to the Ephesians* 20.2.

torment us *before the time*?" (πρὸ καιροῦ).[34] The demons know that
their end is torture and eternal hell, and they wish for it to be *postponed*,
as much as possible, precisely the opposite reaction of the exclamation
"Maranatha," or "Come, O Lord," of the first eucharistic liturgies. Anyone dominated by evil prays for the Kingdom to not come quickly.
Here lies the mystery of freedom in history.[35] With this truth in mind,
St Paul was so preoccupied with the expectation of the Parousia or
Second Coming that he recommended that people not get married,
because he saw that "the appointed time has grown very short,"[36] that
the Kingdom of God was at hand,[37] and he wanted to finish his missionary work in the known world of his time before the Lord's Second
Coming. So, here we see that, thanks to the Resurrection-event, the
future relates to our time in a different way; to be precise, the future
belongs to those who will rise from the grave.

d) *Time as a "measure" of the fact of relation.* In all of creation, only
man can transform time into another temporality, changing time into
kairos. As St Maximus describes it, the *anthrōpos* was introduced last
(ἔσχατος) among beings into space-time for this very reason, so that
he can lead it into the presence and foretaste of the eschaton, as a kind
of natural bond, mediating between the extremities of the universe,
and leading into one the many (other people and creatures) that are
set apart from one another *by an interval*, in order to bring about the
union of everything with God as its cause.[38] In this personal dimen-

---

[34]Mt 8.29.

[35]"Have you not done tormenting me with your accursed time! It's abominable!
When! When! One day, is that not enough for you, one day he went dumb, one day
I went blind, one day we'll go deaf, one day we were born, one day we shall die, the
same day, the same second, is that not enough for you?" Samuel Beckett, "Waiting for
Godot," in *The Complete Dramatic Works* (London: Faber and Faber, 1986), 83.

[36]1 Cor 7.29.

[37]Cf. J. Zizioulas, "Eschatologie et société."

[38]St Maximus the Confessor: "For this reason the *anthrōpos* was introduced last

sion, time does not precede and become an ontologically autonomous and objective dimension, thereby ceasing to be a limitless duration of necessities of causal relations. "If all time is eternally present, all time is unredeemable," notes T. S. Eliot.[39] We cannot "abstract the time in which the thing is," in the words of Douglas Knight, and "see only a flat field without event or interactivity."[40] Time is an event of relationship which precedes as an ontological givenness. In the words of a Russian poet, "nature can have no idea of the past," and from nature's point of view, every new spring is as "fresh as the first spring."[41] Leaves are continually turning yellow, drying up, and falling from the immortal tree of faceless life—but it stands eternally young and indifferent. However, from the *person's* point of view, time "measures" the fact of relation. As a measure of relation, time doubtlessly possesses a certain character of "objectiveness," that is, it should not be conceived merely as a subjective function of the human soul that allows beings to emerge on the "horizon" of consciousness.

However, when a person acts individually, just for himself or herself, completely within the limits of individual need and desire, like the rich fool in the Gospel, forgetting other people, then his or her time ends immediately; his or her day turns to "night."[42] In that case, the person's temporal change is experienced only as an ecstasy of decay, as

---

(ἔσχατος) among beings, as a kind of natural bond (σύνδεσμός τις φυσικός), mediating between the extremities of the universe through its proper parts . . . by an interval . . . *proceeding successively through the intermediate steps by order and rank to God, it receives the end of the lofty ascent through everything occurring by union*" (*Amb.* 41 [PG 91:1305]).

[39]T. S. Eliot, *Four Quartets* (San Diego: Harcourt, 1943), 13.

[40]Douglas Knight, *The Eschatological Economy* (Grand Rapids, MI: Eerdmans, 2006), 181.

[41]See Florovsky, "Utopianism," 88.

[42]This is a very illustrative example, taken from Elder Vasileios of Iveron in his *The Thunderbolt of Ever-Living Fire* (Los Angeles: Sebastian Press, 2014), 47.

a transition to nothingness. And the person hears the voice: "This night your soul is required of you; and the things you have prepared, whose shall they be?"[43] Only love as personal relation can change time into the future's work in progress (as *kairos*). Love is the entrance into the "temporality" of a dimensionless "today," and that constitutes *kairos*.

The Eucharist as Another Temporality

After looking at many (mostly psychological) possible solutions to the problem of time, we turn to concentrate on the Holy Eucharist. As a solution to the problem of time, it contains the following modes: (a) *remembrance* of the future, including Christ's Second Coming and not only his historical life and works; (b) a flight from time into an eternal, authentic temporality of the "present" (πάσαν νῦν ἀποθώμεθα μέριμνα); (c) an affirmation of the past, since it contains the promise that will be fulfilled in the future; and (d) a realization of immortality, since man has been fed with the eucharistic meal.

The Eucharist provides a powerful means of analyzing and clarifying the basic properties of time. It is simultaneously focused on the present, oriented to the future (anticipating consequences), and respectful of the past (memories). It shows how time and space are interwoven in a sort of "cosmic liturgy," in which creation dynamically moves toward its final goal. Actually, of *all temporal categories,* the Eucharist is most frequently described in the Church's hymnography as "today" (σήμερον), the eschatologicial "now." The Eucharist actualizes the nonrepeatable and irreplaceable moments as an enactment,[44] and not as an abstract, timeless formula that contains them.

[43]Lk 12.20.

[44]See the discussion of the problem in William T. Cavanaugh, *Torture and Eucharist: Theology, Politics, and the Body of Christ* (Hoboken, NY: Blackwell, 1998), 234. Cavanaugh asserts, "The Eucharist enacts the presence not simply of what Christ did

However, if this is not understood eschatologically, then the Eucharist ceases to be any of these. In the Eucharist, time is redeemed by the in-breaking of the future into the "present," by a remembrance that implies remembering the future Kingdom (as in the Liturgy of St John Chrysostom), which enables us to see and taste how the world will be at the end, when the Kingdom comes. The Eucharist, thanks to the remembrance as an *enactment*, is a condensed history of the future. Eucharistic time (*kairos*) is a way station from which we can survey the past and look out onto the future. On this basis, ecclesial time is a new chronotype, "justified" by *kairos*.

If eschatology is understood as the redemption of time, which occurs in a surprising way, then the consequences will be felt in our life and the life of society as well. Let us have a closer look at these consequences.

a) *Creation as a prolepsis or foretaste of the end, and as time in the dynamic movement to its blessed "peras."* It is noteworthy that ecclesial time begins with baptism (which is a sacramental death of the "old man"), which reverses the naturalistic perspective of time by putting death at the beginning of new life. This anticipation of the final accomplishment of fullness in Christ by both man and the entire cosmos frees the present from its meaninglessness. This perspective eliminates the desire to escape from time with the help of means such as nihilism, "cryonics," drugs, or forms of entertainment, which have "forgetting" as their goal. At the same time, the ecclesial perspective of time excludes utopianism and any persistent illusion about the past, present, or future. Eschatology presupposes faith in the future through real-time commitment and *ascesis*, which encourages man to heroically endure the sufferings of existence in the present time. It

in the past, but also and especially the future fulfillment of Christ's work through the Spirit."

is thanks to the Eucharist and faith in the Kingdom that the martyrs of the early Church were ready for sacrifice, and not because of some sort of ideology.

b) *Feasts as a redemption of time.* Contemporary man is in a position to see why, for the Church, the eucharistic meal becomes a feast that negates ontological "forgetfulness." Forgetfulness can invalidate every human relationship. This is a characteristic of humans and, according to the Fathers, a grave sin, but not because it is simply a sentimental amnesia. On the contrary, the ecclesial feast, through liturgical, hymnographical, and iconographical commemoration, "molds the memory" of the saint(s). The whole Church "molds the memory" of the saint who is being honored, thereby defying the forgetfulness entailed by created time. Ecclesial "memory" is not merely a sentimental recollection, but the eucharistic community's participation in the "eternal memory," which is in fact the memory in which God the eternal Father—in his pure timelessness—keeps a saint, and, by extension, all the faithful, in eternal existence and communion. Each feast day refreshes the community's relationship with the eschatological being of a saint, indicating the primacy of the future temporality, and revealing another memory (and temporality) that depends on *kairos* rather than *chronos.*

c) *Mysteriological development in Christ.* Another aspect of our discussion about *kairos* is sacramental participation in Christ's life. St Gregory the Theologian developed the idea of *mysteriological* development through Christ's stages. All of Gregory's Christological anthropology is about man's passing through Christ's festal-liturgical path ("travel without fault through every stage and faculty of the Life of Christ").[45] This tradition, different from the Western *imitatio Christi*,

---

[45] *Oration* 38.18 (PG 36:332BC): "Travel without fault through every stage and faculty of the Life of Christ. . . . Lastly, be crucified with Him, and share His Death and

expanded from the time of St Maximus[46] to the epoch of hesychasm, and is based on the conviction that all human life should go through the stages (μεθηλικιώσεις) of Christ.[47] Yet, one must note that St Gregory speaks about the *sacramental* crucifixion of man and his *resurrection* with Christ not in a spiritual vacuum, but in the body of the Church. Without the Church, it is not possible to achieve the retroactive power of Christ's resurrection.

Conclusions: Eucharistic "Real Time" versus the Digital Age

I have discussed here the consequences of eucharistic time not only because I feel certain that they are relatively unknown, but also and perhaps primarily because I want to illustrate some striking new ways of thinking about the ecclesial time in which we live and its implications, which have been a direct result of eschatology.

In an ecclesial context, the problem of time is solved through Pneumatology: the Holy Spirit acts in such a way that time and eternity are not mutually exclusive, so that the past is brought into an existential (and not simply an abstract or a ritualistic) relationship with the present, leaving the present open to the future. But the Holy Spirit is not predictable and is not obliged to follow our linear, horizontal continuity. "Take heed, watch; for you do not know when the time [*kairos*] will come. . . . Watch therefore—for you do not know when

Burial gladly, that thou mayest rise with Him, and be glorified with Him and reign with Him." Cf. Bishop Atanasije Jevtić, "Man in Christ: The Christological Anthropology of St. Gregory the Theologian," in *Emmanuel: The Only Begotten and Firstborn among Many Brethren* (Los Angeles: Sebastian Press, 2008), 67.

[46]St Maximus the Confessor: "The Logos of God, having been born once in the body, according to His will and out of His love for mankind, always gives birth in the Spirit to those who want this" (PG 90:1181).

[47]St Gregory of Sinai: "Whosoever is baptized in Christ should go through all the stages of Christ (τὰς ἐν Χριστῷ μεθηλικιώσεις)" (*The Philokalia* [in Greek], vol. 4:63).

the master of the house will come, in the evening, or at midnight, or at cockcrow, or in the morning—lest he come suddenly [*exaiphnēs*] and find you asleep."[48] Although we know that the grace of God abides in the Church, we nevertheless pray that the Spirit descends and makes real Christ's promises here and now, as if they were not yet completely real.

Now, one may ask if it is possible for a *cause* (an event) that is not from the past but from the future to be at work in the present time. This dilemma is answered by the Bible and the Church—not from our experience of fragmented time in which we creatures exist, but from the anticipation of the eschaton and especially from the Trinitarian teaching of the Fathers. In this perspective, the Eucharist's cause is not merely from something that is established prior (chronologically) to it (i.e., the Last Supper), but primarily from a future event, in other words, from the Kingdom of God.

An ecclesial, neopatristic approach to time helps liberate us from protology (a romantic conception of the past) by offering immanent eschatology as a proposal for life in the present. If every Eucharist is a new event that comes from God through his Spirit, then it is impossible to predict the unfolding of history, as Metropolitan John of Pergamon argues in his paper on eschatology and society.[49] Building on his insights, we can add the following thoughts: the Church cannot share or encourage the arrogance of secular authorities that tend to plan the future of people. To live eschatologically means to allow God to enter history, not only at the end, but at any other moment in time—made possible by the Resurrection as a historic event—thus transfiguring time.

---

[48]Mk 13.33–36.
[49]Zizioulas, "Eschatologie et société."

This vision is both exciting and humbling. The Resurrection of Christ cannot lead to political action to change history; in such a case, it would be, in essence, man who was bringing the eschaton into history.[50] But the most compelling feature of the *ecclesial* chrono-model is the way it incorporates our faith and action. A communion-centered vision, based on the protection of human existential truth and authenticity, can beget a new cultural and ecological paradigm. Eschatology does not leave man inactive, nor does it swallow up history; rather, it frees him from the conviction that what he does corresponds to God's will.[51] How often our actions prove to be completely opposite to God's goals! Examined in the light of eschatology, history is secondary to the judgment of new events, which might or might not approve the previous events, until the last judgment of the Second Coming puts the apocalyptic stamp of final approval or disapproval on human actions in history. Living in an eschatologically conditioned history, Orthodox Christians must issue a new prophetic call for a dialogical theology and the experience of an ecclesial time, which bring us to the journey without end, the journey to the Passover, which is the God-man himself.

That also means that Christian eschatology cannot be accountable for any form of messianism or missionary activity of a zealous type. History is unpredictable precisely because of God's future and the freedom of Yahweh. There must always be a place for God's ultimate and

---

[50]Ibid. On the consequences of this approach for understanding politics, see below in my text "Idealizing Politics Abolishes the Eschaton."

[51]For example: "I hope that makes it understandable that Americans expect their presidents to believe in god. They do so because they are confident that the god presidents believe in is not a god that can call into question the American project. This is why President Obama had to leave his church when his pastor suggested that God might stand in judgment on the US" (Stanley Hauerwas, "How Real is America's Faith?," *The Guardian*, October 16, 2010, http://www.theguardian.com/commentisfree/belief/2010/oct/16/faith-america-secular-britain).

unpredictable judgment regarding our judgments. If all beings have a future, it is not because they have the potential to develop in an Aristotelian sense of "entelechy" or the Omega Point of Teilhard de Chardin's Christology. Human history is not the development or "unfolding" of innate, predetermined inclinations, like the germination and maturation of a seed or the self-realization of a kind of "plan" or "entelechy." The Church does not conceive of and interpret history in teleological categories.[52] All images of the stages (levels, rankings, etc.) in the spiritual life express the dynamism of the trajectory of ecclesial life, but not as something static or unchangeable. However, the future proposed by the Eucharist does not stem from the past, but penetrates into the present by its own initiative, "as a thief in the night." The coming Kingdom does not come "with signs to be observed"[53] but is a free gift from God.[54] From this point of view, salvation is a process that does not depend solely on human efforts. Even in our own days, we encounter penetrating monastic insights into spirituality. But the spiritual life cannot be completely exhausted in a schema of "purification-illumination-perfection," because human life expectancy provides an insufficient time span for achieving salvation. The point is not for there to be chronological progress but to possess an attitude, a relationship that unfolds in time, "allowing a counter-movement of history, not toward the kingdom but rather from the kingdom."[55]

---

[52]If understood as "progressive," the Jewish rectilinear concept of history could be precarious. Those who think that eschatology exists only when there is progress usually forget that it is also progress when one creates a ladder above the abyss, which leads nowhere.

[53]Lk 17.20.

[54]See also the Pauline "in the twinkling of an eye"—ἐν ῥιπῇ ὀφθαλμοῦ (1 Cor 15.52).

[55]J. P. Manoussakis, *God after Metaphysics* (Bloomington, IN: Indiana University Press, 2007), 67.

All this is possible exactly because Christ is the end of the still unconcluded history. Modern physics after Einstein[56] has introduced the notion of "event," which is connected with the existence of the world itself. It could be said that this event is *eschatological* since the entire historical process of the world is tied to the future, the eschaton. That means that the world is created, but ultimately it is not completely created. Thus, *the human being's wholeness can be spoken of only in anticipation.* Man is a real historical and temporal existence, but at the same time, man is not yet what he will be. Man, rather, is not what he is now; he is more what he *will be.*[57]

Each Eucharist is an event introduced in time by the Holy Spirit. That is what the eschatological nature of the Eucharist implies. Orthodox theology emphasizes the *epiclesis* of the Spirit in the Eucharist: the Eucharist makes the expectation of salvation depend not on the historical transmission of the words of institution from the past until today, but on a new action of God in each Eucharist. History does not suffice; a penetration from the future is needed for all new actualizations of the Christ-event. Every aspect of ecclesial life—holiness, sacramental actions, etc.—must allow itself to be tested with regard to whether or not it reflects the meaning warranted by history and the eschatology of Christ.

The Eucharist maintains the dialectical relationship between historical (quantifiable) time (χρόνος) and the transcendent extension of creaturely movement in the eschaton, beyond history. In a society such as ours, which identifies human identity with our "digital" past, the eschatological vision of the Eucharist can have a redeeming effect

---

[56]Einstein confessed that the problem of the "now" (time) worried him seriously. See Rudolf Carnap, "Autobiography," in *The Philosophy of Rudolf Carnap*, ed. P. A. Schilpp (La Salle, IL: Open Court, 1963), 37.

[57]Cf. Bishop Atanasije Jevtić, "Man in Christ," 80.

of great significance. The ethos stemming from that perspective is that we learn to look at all human beings not on the basis of what they were, but as future citizens of the Kingdom of God—as a *foretaste* of the future. Even contemporary thinkers insist that we must reintroduce our capacity to forget.[58] Still, hasn't memory always been long-lasting for some people, such as in cases where individuals are forced out of a community that refuses to forget a major transgression? (The 2012 movie *The Hunt* is a disturbing and unsettling depiction of what happens when a lie becomes the truth, igniting a witch hunt by a society that threatens to destroy an innocent man's life.)[59]

There is hope that this eucharistic model of "remembering" (or, in actuality, of not remembering) is liberating. By experiencing time through the action of the future, man is liberated from slavery to the past, from slavery to facts (from both digital "facts" and naturalistic "fact worship"). If we want to avoid Orwellian issues about the rewriting of history, we need this type of liberation in our time. And this liberation is about the need for repentance. Is it mere chance that our Lord always preached about the coming Kingdom together with the announcement of forgiveness? Thus he created a means for us to place an expiration date on memories we regret. "God does not forgive by announcing that the past is of no account; rather, God makes up what is missing from it,"[60] says D. Knight. And yet, forgiveness is not a juridical term that signifies liberation from sinfulness and punishment. In

---

[58]Cf. Viktor Mayer-Schönberger, *Delete: The Virtue of Forgetting in the Digital Age.*

[59]"It doesn't matter how much they try to accept him. They will never be able to accept him, fully. That is obviously the shot at the end. It's the icing on the cake, in the sense that he can't stay there. He's gotta move on." "Mads Mikkaelsen interview," Collider.com, accessed September 26, 2015, http://collider.com/mads-mikkelsen-the-hunt-hannibal-interview/.

[60]Knight, *Economy*, 24.

this sense, when the future has intervened in our time, then the past does not determine our identity, which means that we are not determined anymore by what we were in the past but by what we will be in the future. The primacy of the future for the historicity of human and cosmic existence is attested to yet again. By offering him the future as a verification of his existence, the Church liberates man from the evil consequences of the past. Therefore, living in a "fore-conception" of the eschaton is a quintessential attribute of ecclesial being, and the Church today must show that this anticipation of the future is constitutive for *all* beings.[61]

---

[61]"[A]t the end of current time, there will remain a kind of spatiality, because of the position of transfigured beings dancing around God, and a sort of temporality, because of the never-ending movement around the divinity. But this eschatological 'space' and 'time' is issued from the divinization, which confers incorruptibility and definitive stability on all reality. This radically new and definitive state of being is called by Maximus an 'ever-well-being.'" Pascal Mueller-Jourdan, "*Where* and *When*," 296.

What Does "Rising from the Dead" Mean?

A HERMENEUTICS OF RESURRECTION

> So you see, you can't be dead. You can't be . . .
> because I love you. You hear me?
> —Trinity, *The Matrix*, directed by the Wachowski brothers

I N *Risen*, a 2016 American biblical drama film directed by Kevin Reynolds, the Resurrection story is recounted by a skeptic who finally meets Yeshua himself. The first forty days after the Resurrection of Jesus Christ are depicted through the eyes of an agnostic Roman centurion, Clavius, authorized by Pontius Pilate to investigate rumors of a risen Jewish Messiah and find the dead body of Jesus of Nazareth to pacify a threatening rebellion in Jerusalem. During his mission, his suspicions of an enigmatic epiphany grow as he encounters the apostles and other historical biblical characters and bears witness to the great events that followed the Resurrection. As his quest to find the body takes him through paradox and disorientation, Clavius uncovers the truth that he's been pursuing. A great mystery unfolds, and he is intensely affected by his first-person investigation, as his previous beliefs about the matter are forever altered based on what he's now witnessed.

Theology's responsibility, in our time and in the time to come, is to give an answer to John the Baptist's question: *Are you he who is to come, or shall we look for another?*[1] For this question is not just for John to ask; this is the question for every generation and age. But that brings us to another question: how does a particular generation and culture recognize Christ as *their* Savior? All these issues can be reduced to the problem of understanding the starting point in theology, to the question of the universal person of Christ. What is it that makes him the only new thing that has ever appeared under the sun? Remember, even though the ancient world knew of the immortality of the soul, the angels, "sons of God," "redeemers," and so on, it had no precedent whatsoever for the mystery of the God-man—the mystery that connects history with eternity and *immortalizes* not just his human nature, but also the entire universe and every individual being.[2]

The answer to the question of how a civilization relates to Christ is interwoven (contextualized) with the intellectual-cultural-ethical milieu of the people who will provide an answer to it. H.-G. Gadamer was right when he categorically stated that understanding always includes historical mediation.[3] However, the issue is not just ethical, intellectual, or aesthetic, but primarily *existential*. Only then it is able

---

[1] Lk 7.19.

[2] "Neither Greco-Roman nor Jewish religious tradition knew about this 'myth'" (Martin Hengel, *The Son of God: The Origin of Christology and the History of Jewish-Hellenistic Religion* [Eugene, OR: Wipf & Stock, 2007], 76). That is why St John of Damascus (*An Exact Exposition of the Orthodox Faith* III.1, ed. Kotter [Berlin and New York: Walter de Gruyter, 1973], 108) said that Christ is "the only new thing under the sun (τὸ μόνον καινὸν ὑπὸ τὸν ἥλιον)," meaning, the only new event in a cyclical context or in the "multiverse." The God-man became *history*, a thing unheard of in the entire ancient world, whose view of history has always been veiled in myth.

[3] Hans-Georg Gadamer, *Truth and Method* (London: Bloomsbury, 2004), 165. This, however, does not imply that the meaning is produced exclusively by the reader in his or her interaction with the text.

to provide responses to the highest pursuits, universal expectations, panhuman anxieties, and deepest requirements of the world, with which Christ is connected in the Spirit. But, first, one thing must be emphasized: Christ is not a *necessary* answer to *all* human demands. He is not even *that king* awaited by the Jews,[4] nor is God how *we* envision him. God in Christ and the Spirit is the One who in his passionate love—even though we do not deserve it—meets us *unexpectedly* in our despair and embraces us when we fall into death.

In order to answer these questions, we begin with an examination of the relationship between the truth (ontology) and human culture (history). In this attempt we will be guided by considerations of modern theology, which seems to introduce the element of futurity, an "eschatology with *eschaton*."[5] And it seems that modern theology uses the resurrection of Christ as a hermeneutical starting point for Christology and anthropology.

The Relationship between the Truth and Human Culture

Let us begin by saying: in order for Christian culture to be an expression of the *ecclesial* ethos emanating from the experience of the Kingdom of God, it must reach beyond its context. Moreover, in a culture/civilization that is determined by rationalism and historicism, it becomes necessary, although extremely difficult, to allow an approach that confirms the factuality of truth by facts—by *events*, to be more precise—that go beyond ephemeral experience, and especially extend to

---

[4]Lk 24.21.

[5]This is as opposed to Heidegger's phenomenology, which seeks in the empirical end of our lives the one and only vantage point to conceive and understand the sense of our being; however, it is an "eschatology without eschaton," as Judith Wolfe points out in *Heidegger's Eschatology: Theological Horizons in Martin Heidegger's Early Work* (Oxford: Oxford University Press, 2013).

the future (eschaton), which the eucharistic community experiences as the Supper of the Kingdom.

Here we become aware of one difficulty. The transcendent cannot be discerned by someone who asserts the truth *exclusively* as *adaequatio rei et intellectus* and never looks beyond the firm boundaries of this realm.[6] Philosophically, truth has traditionally been identified with "reality": what I say—or see—is true because it corresponds with experience. However, since reality is subject to change, corruption, and so on, there is a fundamental and precisely framed question that emerges from such discourse: how can we know what the truth is? Obviously, the definition of truth depends on what you suppose your existence is like, or what your "beholder" eyes expect to see. If somebody told you, "You are dying *now*," then you would say, "That's nonsense." However, when an artist depicts you in a state of dying, he undoubtedly expresses an existential truth. This is exactly the point that Eastern ecclesial art makes with its icon: things that contradict the mind could be more real than those corresponding to it.[7] The iconic ontology does not imply contradiction, since it refers to the reality of the *future*, which is opposed to the reality of Plato, for whom truth is not in the present or future reality but in the ideal world.[8] As modern science is becoming more aware, cosmic harmony and order are more and more

[6] *Transcendental idealism*, a system developed by Kant, is based on the idea that, in order to understand the nature of reality, one must first examine and analyze the reasoning process that governs the nature of experience.

[7] Cf. Fr Maximos Constas's remark: "Only things that contradict the mind are real, there is no contradiction in what is imaginary" (*The Art of Seeing: Paradox and Perception in Orthodox Iconography* [Los Angeles: Sebastian Press, 2014], 31).

[8] See John Zizioulas's remark regarding the Eucharist: "The 'truth of what is now accomplished in the synaxis' is to be found not in a Platonic type of ideal reality but in a 'reality of the future,' in the Kingdom which is to come" (John Zizioulas, *Eucharistic Communion and the World* [New York: T&T Clark, 2011], 44). Also, "the archetype, the cause of 'what is accomplished in the synaxis', lies in the future. The Eucharist is the result of the Kingdom which is to come. The Kingdom which is to come, a future

revealed as objective, *unpredictable*, dynamic happenings that elude "synthetic conclusions" (ruling out definite prediction in the field of physical becoming) and whose workings are incomprehensible to us even though we can distinguish their outlines. It most resembles the paradoxical notion found in quantum physics, that something can be either a particle or a wave, or neither, or something which comprises both, depending how the *other* (observer) perceives it, and whether the other is capable of self-surrender.

Now, if the answers of philosophy, psychology, ethics, and so forth would suffice as a reliable solution, a theologian would not have to turn to Christology. Yet, the context for theological reflection needs the element of *freedom* and of *futurity*, and it can only arise as a result of an *event*. There is reason to believe that the logic hidden in the Resurrection of Christ *verifies* every Christological and ecclesial truth—not as a mere theological *truism*, of course, but as an ontological-hermeneutical answer to the problem of life and death. To understand this point more fully, we must remember that since birth (even from the mother's womb) each person is bestowed with life and the awareness of a dialectic of life and death. A Christology of the Resurrection resolves this dialectic, as we will see explicitly later. The answer, however, is not readily available, but comes rather as a *surprise from the future*: when the case of "the deceiver"[9] was closed after Christ's suffering and death, the Resurrected One entered through a closed door and proclaimed the good news that Life is stronger than death. This opens the door for the Christian epistemology that shows Christ's Resurrection as a *true* event, true precisely because it is so incredible and impossible that no one would dare preach it unless it *de facto* occurred.[10]

event (the state of things to come), being the cause of the Eucharist, gives it its true being" (ibid., 45).

[9] Cf. Mt 27.63.

[10] "The resurrection of Christ must be a true event, because it is, considering

If this is proven correct, then we must accept that, for the Church, the context of the experience of that event is the divine Eucharist, as the *good news* of triumph over death and as an *icon* of the Kingdom. Philosophy, in this case, does not serve as a context but rather as a *tool* for extracting logical implications, while the eucharistic experience serves as the context for becoming cognizant of the existential consequences. The reason for this is that love, knowledge (logic), and faith—within the mystery of theology—cannot be separated.[11]

Dogmas in and of Themselves and Their Relation to Us

While all theological musings on the Resurrection can be compelling, some of them lack a critical sharpness or clarity of description. (If someone uses words like "short," "close," or "excited," we all basically know what is meant, but with the word "resurrection," whose relation with psychological experience is less direct, there are many possible interpretations.) There is an ultimate difficulty that arises from such conversation: should we ascribe a self-evident reality to the Resurrec-

ordinary human expectations, so improbable and impossible that none would have preached it if it had not actually (*de facto*) happened. In other words, if the Apostles had wanted to convince us of some fiction, then, this fiction would have to have been probable, i.e., acceptable to us, so that we could more easily believe in it (is it not the effort of every liar to make his lie seem as convincing as possible just so that the people would more easily believe in it?). But, since the resurrection from the dead is an *extremely improbable* event, and many had, in spite of that, testified about it, then they must have been confronted with irrefutable evidence, otherwise it would never have occurred to them to testify about such a 'foolishness' and 'insanity.'" Vladan Perisić, *Theological Disambiguations: An Unconventional Handbook of Orthodox Theology* (Los Angeles: Sebastian Press, 2012), 23.

[11]Love does not "classify" the experience using some logical principles, because true love does not know the "reluctance" that is present in the epistemological process. "Phenomenology should not and cannot decide *a priori* (i.e., before my relationship with the other and the world) how to classify phenomena, as if it were some old librarian who orders books by their serial number" (Manoussakis, *Metaphysics*, 55).

tion, or should we take it as an *expected* event yet to be confirmed? Long before Gadamer, St Paul introduced the *future* as a hermeneutical tool: "For if the dead are not raised, then Christ has not been raised."[12] The reasoning behind St Paul's conclusion is so subtle that even today it takes a lot of logical effort to appreciate it fully. St Paul intended to indicate that the Resurrection of Christ would become pointless if it were not a collective realization, that is, if the whole body were not implicitly "pre-resurrected" with the Head. The "prehappening" of the future of the world in Christ's Resurrection speaks of the future's work in progress. Obviously, as Pannenberg observes, "Paul's gospel, one must understand, is the exegesis of the appearance of the resurrected Jesus that he experienced."[13] This *a posteriori* verification of the past and of history is almost forgotten in contemporary theology, so it is here that Gadamer steps in with his hermeneutics and dramatically changes the character of the debate. What is the contribution of hermeneutics to our subject? The answer emerges from a simple observation about the importance of the *future*. According to St Maximus the Confessor, who is keen to emphasize the eschaton:

> If. . . everything that was brought from non-being to being is moved because it tends toward some *end*, then nothing that moves is yet at rest. For movement driven by desire has not yet come to rest in that which is *ultimately desirable* (τῷ ἐσχάτῳ ὀρεκτῷ). Unless that which is ultimately desirable is possessed, nothing else is of such a nature as to bring to rest what is being driven by desire (οὐδὲν ἄρα κινούμενον ἔστη, ὡς τοῦ ἐσχάτου μήπω τυχὸν ὀρεκτοῦ).[14]

[12]1 Cor 15.16.

[13]Wolfhart Pannenberg, *Jesus—God and Man* (Philadelphia: Westminster, 1977), 73.

[14]*Ambiguum* 7.3 (PG 91:1069B). According to Maximus the creation occurs out of the future so that the beginning of creation is inconceivable without the future

If we take hermeneutics[15] seriously and, to recall St Maximus' logic, we are surprised by the fact that there is nothing that is not *interpretable by the future*, then there is "nothing" behind; nothing is the past. This is a radically strange reality: it is only in the *distance of the future* that the mystery of existence (and, clearly, of salvation) will appear evident. Everything that is behind us, we have lived it as "today," and only by living it in that way, as today, does it receive its meaning. In other words, the future substantiates history in an ontological way. Only after the Resurrection did the disciples "remember His words."[16]

The "logic of the Resurrection" differs from the classical scholastic approach in a number of essential ways, and foremost for us are the following three points.

The first one is related to the reality of *death*. Although the joy of life is truer than the agony of death that accompanies it, one cannot live the Resurrection without experiencing the tragedy of death. Even the saints die.

---

end. St Maximus' interpretation is markedly different from that of Origen (see my article "The Beginning and the End Are not the Same" in this book, fn. 28) and St Gregory of Nyssa: "In the case of the first creation the final state was intertwined with the beginning (ἐπὶ μὲν οὖν τῆς πρώτης κτίσεως ἀδιαστάτως τῇ ἀρχῇ συνανεφάνη τὸ πέρας) and the race took the starting point of its existence in its perfection (καὶ ἀπὸ τῆς τελειότητος ἡ φύσις τοῦ εἶναι ἤρξατο)." See also: ". . . it was the case for each of these that its start and its full actualization were achieved together (ἐφ᾽ ἑκάστου τῶν ὄντων ἀδιαστάτως τῇ ἀρχῇ συναπηρτίσθη τὸ πέρας). . . . [F]or all that were brought from nonexistence to existence their perfection coincided with their beginning (πᾶσι τοῖς ἐκ τοῦ μὴ ὄντος εἰς τὸ εἶναι παραγομένοις ὁμοῦ τῇ ἀρχῇ συνανασχούσης τῆς τελειότητος) . . . from its first moment of existence it was formed simultaneously with its perfection (ἀπὸ τῆς πρώτης ὑπάρξεως συμπλασθεῖσα τῇ τελειότητ)" (St Gregory of Nyssa, *Commentary on Song of Songs* 15.5, *GNO* 6:486).

[15]Hermeneutics here is not a process in which an interpreter finds a particular meaning, but a creative effort to account for understanding as the ontological process of man.

[16]Lk 24.8.

Second, the fact that there will be a resurrection of the body demonstrates that the *future* is quintessential. This dimension of the *future* has sadly disappeared from the horizon of contemporary theologians, as they consider everything to have been solved. Even in the Orthodox milieu people tend to take it for granted that the saints are "fine" now. However, when the Church sings, "death is trampled down by death," it points to the *future*, to something that *will* be revealed. So, we can only anticipate or, eucharistically, foretaste it.

The third one is related to *expectation*. This problem comes to the surface more and more because there is a great tendency today to replace the notion of "foretaste" with the idea of the "realization" of the eschaton. We do not deny that there is a "real presence" (for instance, Christ's presence in the Eucharist), but we have to add one caveat, since we await that happening as a reality in the future. It doesn't take too much effort to recognize a paradoxical structure in history and, particularly, in biblical history: (a) the future "precedes" the past; (b) everything that happens is not completed in the moment of its happening but has its meaning in the future; (c) one must *wait* if he or she wants to see that which has happened; and (d) if the future does not come to show what it was that has happened, then it (the past event) has no meaning and, literally, does not exist. From this perspective, the future is more than just an aspect of time; in the Bible, time is the future's work in progress.

Unfortunately, this element of *expectation* (προσδοκία) and *prolepsis* has almost disappeared from contemporary theology,[17] as if we do

---

[17]It is with a sense of relief that we come across a renowned Protestant theologian who identifies this problem and discusses it. "Where the tension between the present and the expectation for the future is lost, the occurrence of Jesus' resurrection loses the inherent significance that it originally had, that is, the significance that was inherent in it within its original context in the history of traditions, namely, in the horizon of the apocalyptic expectation for the future" (Pannenberg, *Jesus*, 66–67).

not need to wait. This is an important topic in theology. In our modern debate, the notion of "realized eschatology" has to be corrected. But how can this be done? Oscar Cullman has a solution, and the answer he found is a logical yet profound extension of our discussion so far. The famous phrase that he invented to describe this dialectic is very important: the Kingdom is *already* here, but *not yet*. This concept has important implications. For example, we should not be satisfied with seeing a saint merely as a *relic* but should also desire to see them alive, which, again, leads us to the *future*. We should be concerned with death. When we stop being concerned with death—and with the expectation of its destruction—our creativity dries out. Precisely from the struggle with death spring love, sacrifice, art, and so on.

To understand this point more fully, accept for a moment that dogmas are relevant only in the sense that their truth and validity are applicable *to us*. In this case, there is no danger, then, that the transcendent side of dogmas could be mistaken for their contextual expression as long as the transcendence of truth is a reality which is *yet to come* and be manifested in its fullness. Paradoxically, *the transcendent mystery of dogmas acts most powerfully not from the past* (for example, in the world of Ideas), *but rather from the future*.[18] By the power of the Holy Spirit, dogmas are exposed through "anamnesis," but not merely in the "psychological-experiential" sense. The Holy Spirit actualizes the nonrepeatable and irreplaceable moments as a "prolepsis"[19] or an

---

[18]This approach is somehow at odds with the "protological" sentence in the well-known saying in the *Epistle of Barnabas*, "Behold, I make the last things as the first things" (Barn 6.13). What is meant by this is that "only the one who has control over the beginning has the whole matter in his grasp. The beginning therefore had to be illuminated by the end, and ultimately the idea of pre-existence was a favorite means of bringing out the special significance of particular phenomena for salvation" (Hengel, *Son of God*, 69).

[19]"The thing that often escapes us is that, in the New Testament, the Spirit is given after Christ's Resurrection (Jn 7.39), precisely because his coming into the world sig-

enactment, and not as an abstract, timeless *formula* that would contain them. Fr Matthew Baker's approach—in which he successfully encompassed Florovsky, Pannenberg, and Zizioulas, to mention a few—is one of the most attainable proposals about the dogmas put forward in the last fifty years. Baker was vexed about the Tillichian echo in the discussion about the "existential concern."[20] We can add that dogmas, in fact, are genuine only in the sense that their truth and validity, which are truly *eschatological*, have always been active and present in the *mystery* (for the eschaton allows the human experience to take its course in history and does not deny it). In this context we are reminded of the unavoidable messianic *anticipation* of the dogmas of the Incarnation and the Resurrection of Christ in the Old Testament. Pannenberg rightly observed, "Why the man Jesus can be the ultimate revelation of God, why in him and only in him God is supposed to have appeared, remains incomprehensible apart from the horizon of the apocalyptic expectation."[21]

nals the coming of the 'last days' in history (Acts 2.17). It is no exaggeration to identify the Kingdom and the Holy Spirit: 'Thy Kingdom come: that is, the Holy Spirit.' So the linking of the Holy Spirit with 'holding together the whole institution of the Church' suggests that both the 'institution' of the Church and the framework within which it becomes a reality, the eucharistic synaxis in other words, derive their meaning from the Kingdom of God." Zizioulas, *Eucharistic Communion and the World*, 74.

[20] In his comments on the discussion of the "answer" and the "concern," Matthew Baker wrote that it sounds very Tillichian, and insisted on the stability of the *content* of the message, which Florovsky so stressed. For Baker, "The concern is human, but the message is divine. And the condition for apprehending and understanding the message is not simply a universal human concern, but precisely *faith*—which again is a divine gift" (unpublished correspondence). According to Pannenberg (*Jesus*, 73), "The unity of event and word in the resurrection appearances is important for the question of how this event can establish faith. If the resurrection or the appearances of the resurrected Jesus were only brute facts without inherent significance, then, certainly, the origin of faith would not be understandable from this event. But that event had its own meaning within its sphere in the history of traditions."

[21] Pannenberg, *Jesus*, 83.

Once again, this idea of the "future's work in progress" is strongly suggested by a number of well-reasoned considerations, and we should take a look at some of the most prominent. In the eucharistic experience of the Resurrection as the true judgment of this world, the Church validates dogmatic paradoxes, which no epistemology can comprehend without the element of *freedom* (freedom to *relate*), because these dogmas are a *remembrance of the future*. Thus, historically, dogmas are not "stages" of the Christological teaching that lead to an end (volition-creation-perfection); on the contrary, the *apocalyptic* nature of time, as the Church understands it, allows for, guarantees, and makes possible the *sudden* (ἐξαίφνης) penetration of the Truth "always and in all things."[22] So, the apocalyptic nature of ecclesial *kairos* breaks with the classic Greek tradition.[23] Zizioulas's arguments regarding a *remembrance of the future* consider some concrete forms of ecclesial communion that reflect this. First, "remembering" something that has not yet happened (the Second Coming) cannot be explained unless it is transferred to an existential plane on which the fragmentation and necessary sequence of the three elements of time (past, present, and future) have been healed. Second, in the Kingdom everything is not turned into "present" but into the "future age which does not end or grow old," which, being the state that ultimately prevails, is logically prior, since it is this that gives "substance" and meaning to both past and present. Third, the "end" constitutes the "reason" for which both the past and the present "subsist," according to St Maximus. In consequence, the future age that does not end, Zizioulas holds, becomes not

[22]"For the Word of God . . . wants always and in all things to accomplish the mystery of His embodiment." St Maximus the Confessor (PG 91:1084CD).

[23]Yet, we naturally ask, how can God possibly behave in such a strange manner? The answer is that in no way can we control or predict the outcome of any "spiritual" action. We cannot ever know the exact location of God's presence. We cannot predict with total certainty the outcome of even the simplest of spiritual moments.

an effect, like something that happens in time as we know it after the fall, but the *cause* of all past and present events. Finally, *remembrance* of this "endless" future is not only possible but also ontologically definitive in the realm of the Eucharist as an icon of the Kingdom.[24]

In keeping with the futurity principle, though, is the Christological question the same for each age? According to epistemic contextualism, the answer is no. If, nonetheless, it goes beyond epistemology and includes the element of freedom, the Christological question is then *the same* for all ages, since it deals with *being* and *nonbeing*: Jesus Christ saves the world from nonexistence—and does it only as a perfect God and a perfect Man in the Person of the Logos Incarnate and Resurrected.

To one extent or another, this view of the Resurrection-logic is one that many of us hold, if only implicitly. However, a necessary assumption of the existential significance of the Resurrection is that the Church "vivifies" dogmas, which implies that Christ becomes the way of being only *within* the ecclesial life. This could be an important realization for all of us: Outside the realm of the Church, teachings are mere "dogmas," that is, mere semantic-logical propositions, "surpassing all logic" for those who believe and "illogical" for those who do not believe. Without freedom and outside the Church, Christological dogmas are applicable only to Jesus Christ, but they do not then have the power to raise the mortal to the immortal. Fr Georges Florovsky developed this idea in particular:

> For the erring Christian consciousness, what is characteristic is precisely this striving for a logical exhaustion of faith, as if striving for a substitution of the living communication with God by

[24]See Zizioulas, *Eucharistic Communion and the World*, 59–60. Zizioulas claims that "this is attested both in the Gospel descriptions of the Last Supper and in the liturgical practice of the Church" (ibid).

religious and philosophical speculations about the Divine, of
life—by teaching. . . . [I]n the need to fetter all the fullness of
Church experience and hope into an infallible system of final dogmatic definitions, there is expressed a certain historical docetism,
a derogation of the reality of time, a derogation of the mystery of
the Church, derogation of the future Coming in glory—one might
say, a bad remnant of time, in which the real "deification" of creation and development in grace is replaced by a logical unfolding
of timeless and abstract principles.[25]

It turns out that the purification of all redundant contextual "depos-
its" for the sake of overcoming the naturalistic idolatry is necessary
in order to gain the "one thing needful,"[26] which is knowledge of the
Conqueror of death.

The apostles passed on the truth of the Resurrection to the Church
that, particularly during eucharistic gatherings, reveals and celebrates
this greatest Christological event. This event—the Resurrection of
Jesus Christ, the God-man and Savior of the world according to the
faith of the Church—now, paradoxically, *precedes* all other events or
doctrines, including the Incarnation. (The Cappadocian Fathers and
St Maximus support this assertion.)[27] The Resurrection of the Messiah
who rose from the dead "historically" (and not just rhetorically) precedes all other events, which now become resurrectional projections
and consequences.[28]

[25]George Florovsky, "The House of the Father," in *Ecumenism I: A Doctrinal Approach*, vol. 13 of *The Collected Works of Georges Florovsky* (Büchervertriebsanstalt, 1989), 84.

[26]Cf. Lk 10.42.

[27]Cf. St Gregory the Theologian, *Or.* 45.22; St Maximus, *Or. Dom.* (PG 90:879D–880B); etc. The Resurrection clarifies, at least in St Maximus' account, the exact onto-logical import of the Incarnation into the history of salvation.

[28]"All things in Christology are judged in the light of the resurrection. . . . This is

Truth and the Resurrection of Christ

What, then, is the essence, basis, or *prototype* of dogma? Is it its theoretical or "logical" core, or is it something else? Gadamer gives priority to the "original" vis-à-vis its interpretation.[29] But what solution to this dilemma is offered by Orthodox Christian tradition and theology?

The answer to this question comes from the Resurrection of Christ as an event and the human response to it. As seen in the light of the New Testament, the event of the Resurrection of Christ is the foundation of all dogmas, and no dogma can be understood or explained *in itself*, outside of this *event* and its relation to *it*. Christology (and theology in general) is existentially irrelevant if death, as the basic problem of creation, is not *overcome*. Christology is about the following question: Who is Jesus Christ for every particular existential condition, for each epoch, and not just for the apostolic age? It is not possible to answer this question on the basis of ephemeral human desires and opinions, but only on the basis of soteriological expectations and resources (existential concepts, images, manners) available to the spiritual world in any given situation. Neither the *analogia entis* of the Scholastics nor Spinoza's "intellectual love of God" can help in this matter. It requires an *event* that ontologically joins the created with the Uncreated, an *event* that breeds hope for overcoming death, the longing for true life, in all creation.

The opening of our eyes to the true nature of the Resurrection has always been one of theology's primary purposes. Those who accept the

the way in which Christology in the New Testament has developed—from the resurrection to the incarnation, not the other way around—and patristic theology has never lost this eschatological approach to Christology." John Zizioulas, *Being as Communion* (Crestwood, NY: St Vladimir's Seminary Press, 1985), 55n49.

[29]"Interpretation does not seek to replace the interpreted work. It does not, for example, seek to draw attention to itself by the poetic power of its own utterance." Gadamer, *Truth and Method,* 418.

"logic" of the Resurrection are obliged to follow the argument wher-
ever it leads, to paraphrase the words of Socrates in Plato's *Republic*.
The Resurrection means and reveals everything the Holy Scripture
says about it: that God the Father raised his eternal Son by the Holy
Spirit; through this event, the ontology of the world and matter has
experienced a radical change. Each movement of the paschal mystery
thus attests to the mystery of Sonship.[30] As we'll discuss later, the exis-
tential-logical premise of the Christology of the Resurrection means
that only the Life-creating Trinity can restore the original foundation
of the person, that is, redeem existence. As Fr Matthew Baker pointed
out, "the Resurrection and the Kingdom of God form the chief context and condition for historical understanding," by adding a crucial
(and in some way programmatic) assertion, "Christian theology is *a
hermeneutics of resurrection*—the ever-new understandings of a cloud
of witnesses in every age arising and entering permanently into the
body of truth."[31]

In this sense, then, all other dogmas (truths) of Christianity are
simply *reflections* or expressions of the dogma of the Resurrection.
From then onward, we can understand the overall mystery of existence
only in retrospect, as the Cappadocians and St Maximus the Confessor

---

[30]Anne Hunt, "The Trinity Through Paschal Eyes," in *Rethinking Trinitarian Theology: Disputed Questions And Contemporary Issues in Trinitarian Theology*, ed. G.
Maspero and R. Wozniak (New York: T&T Clark, 2012), 480. "In and through the
post-resurrection shock waves, the disciples recognize Jesus as Lord and God, the
Father as author of this plan for our salvation, and the Holy Spirit as yet another divine
power centre in their new God-consciousness, not merely a divine impersonal force
but a distinct personal being, one in whom Father and Son are united in love" (ibid.,
486).

[31]Fr Matthew Baker, "'Alles Verständnis ist Interpretation': Neo-Patristic Synthesis and Philosophical Hermeneutics—Georges Florovsky and Hans-Georg Gadamer
in Conversation" (unpublished paper, 2012). Baker's paper can now be viewed as
among the first to point out the "resurrection hermeneutics."

emphatically claimed.[32] Not even a vision of the transfigured Lord was sufficient to fathom the mystery of Christ, and that is why the evangelist wrote: "He charged them to tell no one what they had seen, *until the Son of man should have risen from the dead.* So they kept the matter to themselves, questioning what the rising from the dead meant."[33] The apostles had not yet become aware of the true problem. Only in the light of the Resurrection—which is the solution to the eternal life of creation—could they see the true *problem* of the created world.[34] Asserting the retroactive power of the Resurrection, Pannenberg states:

> [O]nly an integrated view of the Easter event together with the coming end, a view originally based on the expectation of the eschatological imminent end, made it possible to understand Jesus' activity and fate as God's revelation. An individual event can say something about the one God only when it has in view the totality of reality. In the Biblical sense, however, *this totality as the totality of history is accessible only through the anticipation of the end of all events.*[35]

[32]"Moreover, the entire season of Pentecost is a reminder of the *resurrection* we expect in *the age to come*" (St Basil the Great, *On the Holy Spirit* 27.66); "Thus the honoring of the number seven brought with it the honor of Pentecost. For seven multiplied by itself generates fifty minus one day, and this we have taken from the age to come, which is at once the eighth and the first (Gen. 1:5; John 20,1.26), or rather one and indissoluble" (St Gregory the Theologian, *Or.* 41.2 [SC 358, 316–18; PG 36:432AB]). St Maximus the Confessor adds that this "state *above nature* (καὶ γενέσθαι ἐν τῇ ὑπὲρ φύσιν) is identified with the Eighth day (ἥτις ἐστὶν ὀγδόη) and characterizes the future condition (καὶ τὴν μέλλουσαν χαρακτηρίζει κατάστασιν)" (*Quaestiones et dubia* 191 [CCSG 10:133]; cf. also *Letter to Marinos* [PG 91:81D]).

[33]Mk 9.9–10.

[34]"For Western theology as a whole, the resurrection of Christ is nothing more than a confirmation of the saving work of the cross. The essential part has already been accomplished in the sacrifice on the cross." Zizioulas, *Eucharistic Communion and the World*, 39–40.

[35]Pannenberg, *Jesus*, 185 (our emphasis).

This is a deep and subtle suggestion. To really absorb it, we need to put ourselves into the example earnestly and fully imagine the experience of the apostles. The testimony of the apostles about the resurrected Christ is the first dogmatic "formulation" and verification of the truth about God: there is a God who is powerful enough to conquer death. For the apostles, the Resurrection of Jesus was proof that he was the eschatological Messiah, the true *anthrōpos*, who, in contrast to the first Adam, took the world in his hands with thanksgiving and offered it back to God, freeing creation from the bondage of sin/death, thus setting not only the *end* but also the *beginning* (ἀρχή) of the world. The same is valid for St Paul. When he realized that Jesus—whom he persecuted—was no longer dead, his worldview was completely turned upside down: if Jesus was exalted by God in his resurrection, then his *death* must have had a *meaning* in God's economy. According to Pannenberg,[36] there are several points that summarize the immediate inherent significance of Jesus' Resurrection. First, if Jesus has been raised, then the end of the world has begun. Second, if Jesus has been raised, this can only mean, for a Jew, that God himself has confirmed the pre-Easter activity of Jesus. Third, through his Resurrection from the dead, Jesus so closely resembled the Son of Man that the insight became obvious to St Paul: the Son of Man is none other than the man Jesus who will come again. This is a key realization: if Jesus, having been raised from the dead, has ascended to God, and if thereby the end of the world has begun, then God is ultimately revealed in Jesus. As a cultural implication, the transition to the gentile mission is then motivated by the eschatological Resurrection of Jesus as the Resurrection of the Crucified One.[37]

[36]Ibid., 67–73.

[37]In spite of the occasional inconsistencies in Pannenberg's priority of futurity (neglect of the *somatic* aspect as constitutive of the meaning of a person, insistence

This reasoning is sound, as far as it goes, since each age does *not* begin its search for God from some eternal principle (πρωταρχικὴ ἀρχὴ) that it tries to understand or interpret, but from the thirst for the resurrected life, from making the Resurrection present in the Church through the Eucharist: there, Christians come to know God by fostering a *relationship* with him and not by grasping the meanings of some unalterable, abstract, divine concepts. Furthermore, every age interprets this experience (event) within its own context. The Greek Fathers interpreted this event with the assistance of the ontological questions of philosophy (i.e., the ontological problem). They received the Semitic (in this case, iconic) version of the truth of the Incarnation and the Resurrection, but they interpreted it ontologically by using Greek idioms. They are the ones who established the doctrines so that a *simple* (Semitic) religion might have a *systasis* (σύστασις), or ontological content.[38] With this approach, the Fathers brought a shift in perspective, enabling us to rediscover the true meaning of iconicity in history.

This leads us to the concluding point in our understanding of the problem. Since our civilization and culture are essentially still "Hellenic," because they are based on the Greek philosophical heritage with its interest in ontology (the question "What truly *is*?" originated in Greece), we can therefore say with Florovsky that the "Hellenism" of the Church is a diachronic, permanent category. Of course, it is not advisable to insist that the cultures of Africa, China, or any other place should adopt "Hellenism," because these cultures express their interest in salvation through iconology and symbols different from those

that the only divine Thou in Jesus' earthly life was the Father, etc.), his contribution to Christology is substantial.

[38]". . . in simple words through the power of the Spirit, you *framed dogmas* (συνιστάτε τὰ δόγματα) set down earlier by the fishermen . . . indeed our plain faith needed a *consistency* (τὴν σύστασιν)." *Kontakion of the Holy Three Hierarchs*, in Greek Menaion (PG 29:369A).

required by Hellenic terminology, which is based on the ontological questions of being, life, and death. What can and should be accepted by these or any other cultures is the Resurrection-of-Christ event, which can link Christ with their own essential issues. Thus the folk art of those cultures will inevitably manifest the resurrected ethos, just as—following the logic of the Resurrection—Christian iconography from the beginning depicted a *risen* man, adding a crown of light as a sign of adoption and the resurrectional relationship with the transcendent God.[39] How did this happen? In contrast with natural art that idealizes the natural world and is therefore bounded by time, the icon is the truth presented in a way that is not controlled by our senses or our mind; you cannot conceive it. This encounter with the divine, in paradox and ambiguity, is a matter of *relation* rather than logical argumentation. Since our relation in history is also iconic, not direct (this perceived "weakness" of the icon is precisely its "strength"), we cannot have logical proof; rather, there is a decision one makes to *relate*.[40]

In this sense, every culture, despite the ongoing cultural *constants* characteristic of all ages, has its own "mindset" by which to evaluate the authority of the truth revealed to it. The reasoning of Florovsky, Pannenberg, and Zizioulas can easily be extended to the question of how eternal *truth* becomes relevant for different "mindsets." As already noted, for Semitic culture, it is essential that the truth be revealed by someone who *lives (does) the truth*—doing (πράττειν) takes priority over being (εἶναι)—hence the extreme asceticism of the Stylites, for example. Jewish culture expects the truth from someone who brings

[39]Cf. Stamatis Skliris, *In the Mirror: A Collection of Iconographic Essays and Illustrations* (Los Angeles: Sebastian Press, 2007), 101.

[40]Therefore, the iconic approach presupposes that one accepts a presence to which one can *relate*. This was the argumentation of the theologians (among them, St Maximus the Confessor, St John Damascene, and St Theodore the Studite) throughout the history of Byzantium.

the judgment of history (hence, apocalypses as a test for the truth-fulness of history), whereas Greek culture looks for someone who is eternal, who is verily the only truth. If there is *one* answer to all that searching across all cultures and ages, it is the *Resurrection*. It is the *constant* and unchanging condition *sine qua non* of every soteriology. Upon hearing "Christ is risen" from the myrrh-bearing women, the Jew understands it as the beginning of judgment upon all, the Greek as a victory over corruptibility, the Chinese as the eternal Tao, and the postmodern man—perhaps?—as his human *right* to deification. The point, however, is that this truth should not be merely proclaimed but lived in the faith, at which time our being will then resound as it shouts, "Christ is risen!" (This also eliminates the issue of the clarity of what we are proclaiming.) For Christ not only solves the problem of simple being (and its ethical-aesthetic or juridical dilemma), but gives an *eternal well-being* (ἀεὶ εὖ εἶναι), because he is the bearer of immortality, incorruption, and the perpetuation of existence.

Implications of a Hermeneutics of Resurrection

The neopatristic insights of the twentieth and twenty-first centuries have generated excitement because they have raised the possibility of a new answer—one in which Tradition plays a crucial role in interpretation, pointing back toward the Greek Fathers and their hermeneutics, and advocated by Florovsky, Zizioulas, John Behr, and others. In this perspective, the preaching of the Resurrection is the nucleus of every dogma. "Christ is risen" is the message for all people, but the Greeks give the reply: "*Truly* he is risen!" The incarnate Christ overcame death, thus showing the correlation between *truth* and *existence*, something that would be recognized by the apostles only *after* the Resurrection, not before. In his Person, the created lives forever, and the Holy Eucharist, as the resurrectional event *par excellence*, is a guarantor of this.

This hermeneutics is among the most precious and monumental achievements of the Greek Fathers. It should be emphasized at this point that Hellenism is not some independent, eternal category, but one important, spiritual category that served as a key requirement for the *universality* of the Church. In relation to the Church, Hellenism is not an independent value uncritically inherited by the Church Fathers. Hellenism had to be transformed by the same Fathers.

We then reach the most important point of this argument. The essence of Christology is not in itself, but in its existential "transformation" and "topos," which is the Church. In "itself" (i.e., without ecclesiological realization), Christology is simply a "dogma" without existential significance: it explains something that is applicable to Jesus Christ (for example, the Incarnation), but not to all of us. Even for a believing Christian, if it is separated from the Church's community, a dogma is a "supralogical" proposition that is believed without argument solely because it is a "dogma." "In its ecclesiological significance, however," as Zizioulas remarked (after previously considering what the Chalcedonian terms "without division" and "without confusion" mean outside the experience of the Church), "this dogma expresses a way of being."[41] Only this relationship can indicate the logical or philosophical (primarily in the analytical sense) aspects of the dogma of Christ and the Holy Trinity, and never vice versa.

In conclusion, let us add the following to those considerations: What Christ reveals through his Person is an unprecedented way of two natures existing in his hypostasis, a way that mysteriously leads into ecclesiology. St Maximus, along with the great Fathers of the monastic tradition, such as St Macarius, demonstrated that the God-man capti-

[41]John Zizioulas, *Communion and Otherness* (New York: T&T Clark, 2006), 261.

vates with the countenance that reveals and radiates the unfathomable eschatological newness of Love who once was lifted up to the Cross, descended to Hades, and was resurrected from the grave. Therefore, the Church has no definition of truth that simply satisfies intellectual curiosity; any aspiring definitions must describe a life experience, like the famous definition of Nicholas Cabasilas: "The Church is seen (present) in the holy mysteries" (and especially in the Eucharist).[42]

We thus understand here that a dogmatic "gigantomachia" does not simply end in the agreement of words and formulas, but in the reality of the Mystery, recognized in the image of the crucified and resurrected Christ.[43] Then, by his ethos, the Church can daringly struggle in history and, although realistically weak, be victorious; being defeated, crushed, humiliated, it is able to encourage the defeated, resurrect the dead, and in the arena of history appear "in another form,"[44] and exist even where it phenomenologically "is not." To this, as well as to the victory of dogmas, testify the Church Fathers, who bear that name exactly because they help us be born again in the community of the Holy Spirit.

With these seemingly slight modifications, our understanding of theology's arena is transformed. The eternal truths of the Church's

---

[42]"The Church is present in the Holy Mysteries (the Eucharist) not in symbols but as members of the heart. . . . For this is not a fellowship in name only, or some similarity by analogy, but this is the very same (identical) thing. For these mysteries are the Body and the Blood of Christ, and they are the real food and drink of Christ's Church. . . . And if someone could see Christ's Church through the extent of one's unity with Christ and through the communion with His Body, he would see none other than only the Body of Christ." Nicholas Cabasilas, *Commentary on the Liturgy* 38.43, 45 (PG 150:452–53, 461–65).

[43]An icon bridges the chasm between Creator and creation only through the intervention of the *Person* of Christ, as opposed to pagan symbolism, which believes that *nature* bridges the chasm on its own.

[44]Mk 16.12.

experience come to us revived with a new infusion of creativity. The way is new, but not the content; we are not talking about new things, but about the same in a new, different way. Christ asks us again, "But who do you say that I am?" The answer cannot but read exactly like Peter's: "You are the Christ, the Son of the living God."[45] The question is who will ask the question and who will provide the answer.

The mission and the calling of the Church are to foster the hermeneutics of the Resurrection as something that speaks to all people and all contexts. Our theology, a eucharistic vision of the world, has preserved and upheld this truth throughout history, but it has to continue to do so into the future, in our millennium. Only as such will it bring hope and life to the world.

[45]Mt 16.15–16.

"We Have Passed out of Death into Life"

REFLECTIONS ON THE FEAR OF DEATH

> If we can imagine our own deaths but still manage to come
> back to life, then it proves that we can survive anything.
> —Narrator, *The Family Fang*, directed by Jason Bateman

I N HIS INTRIGUING NOVEL, *Death with Interruptions*, the Por-
tuguese author and Nobel Prize winner Jose Saramago imagines
what would happen if Death decided there would be no more death.
The story begins at the stroke of midnight on New Year's Eve of an
unspecified year, when the people of an undisclosed country suddenly
stop dying. People now weaken but never quite pass away, and no one
knows why. Naturally, this causes bewilderment among politicians,
doctors, funeral directors, and religious leaders. The general public,
on the other hand, initially celebrates this sensational news—flags are
hung out on balconies, people dance in the streets. Humanity's great
goal—eternal life—has been achieved. Despite that, the new reality
starts to hit home—families are left to care for the permanently dying,
life insurance policies become meaningless, and funeral parlors are
reduced to arranging burials for pet dogs, cats, hamsters, and parrots.

As Saramago's novel shows, our age is enigmatic. In spite of its resemblance to other epochs and their behaviors, it is distinguished by a *condensed* mode of existence that navigates an ever-increasing velocity, stratification, and deluge of information. This new way of life, which is both adopted by and imposed on us, accelerates us toward a crisis of the paradigm of the culture of modernity, which no longer meets man's needs, despite all its high-gloss accomplishments. The condensed quality of our culture in crisis alters how we perceive the constituent elements of human existence (love, freedom, fear, death, illness, etc.) and our sense of both space and time. One aspect of this changing perception is the different ways in which the anxiety of death, with its raw, ugly uniformity, is experienced. These variations of experience include death anxiety and concerns over mortality, making "the fear of death" a many-faceted subject. As much as death is an unavoidable fact, it is a vexing mystery too, open to different interpretations and experiences. As something holy, it is *mysterium fascinandum et tremendum*. As a terror, it frightens and even creates severe, irrational fear (known as *thanatophobia*) in acute cases.

These various modes of perceiving the fear of death in our culture challenge the Church, which proclaims both the horror of death (humanity's enemy) and Christ's victory over it (Christ's Resurrection). The Church recognizes that *thanatophobia* is a fairly complex and *justified* phobia, since it is a fear of the real and final enemy of all creatures, death. All humans, the God-man in Gethsemane included, were afraid of dying. Without any pretense, Christ hated death. He never preached acceptance of death, but rather the Passover or Pascha, which goes *beyond* death and fear, since there can be no reconciliation between life and death. On the other hand, death was trampled down. From a biological point of view, death opposes, contradicts, and denies human beings' primary *eros* (desire) for existence and survival.

It is clear that every generation and age has a similar fear of death as its chief feature; there is something constant, unchanging in this phenomenon. Truly, death defines us, and fear is its symptom. This *phobia* is actually even the measuring device of history. Yet, the fear of death is deeper than a mere psychological emotion, for death is above all an ontological fact. Its annihilating hand stretches out and threatens our very being with nothingness, inciting an irresolvable terror leading to the narcissism of death. There is a debate about whether the *death penalty* (the sentence of death given to a person as a punishment for a serious offense by judicial process) is one of the most *effective* deterrents against criminal behavior, thus maintaining order in society. (Although it does raise the question: how can the death penalty serve the law when it completely eliminates both the purpose and subject of the law, the human person?) In addition, as the Bible says, "For fear has to do with punishment, and he who fears is not perfected in love."[1]

Still, when considering the fear of death, it must be emphasized that the theoretical context cannot be divorced from the *practical* aspect. Death is a tragic, practical problem, especially when related to illness. Death, fear, and illness are indeed the three symptoms of our relation to nothingness. It is not by accident that both philosophers and Christian ascetics elaborated on *memento mori*, μνήμη θανάτου. Death, in conjunction with fear (and, sometimes, illness), marks and shapes both our bodies and our culture. All our fears and reflections on death thus follow us around like an underlying musical motif, sometimes rising to a crescendo and sometimes quieting to *pianissimo*. This near-constant "remembrance of death" can be *unwilling* (and the culture *has* to deal with it) or *voluntary* (as in monasticism). Either way, Epicurus captures the inevitability of death when he writes, "Against all else it is possible to provide security, but as against death all of us mortals

[1] 1 Jn 4.18.

alike dwell in an unfortified city."[2] Although an undetermined and indefinable being, man is clothed in "garments of skins" (δερμάτινοι χιτῶνες),[3] and his body is the *locus* of this conflict. St Paul fearfully asks, "O wretched man that I am! Who will deliver me from this body of death?"[4] We tend to think that our bodies are fortified cities protecting our "selves" from any intrusion, but eventually we realize that they are instead what we use to protect our "selves" from the rays of Truth, to which even death is subordinate.

This is the precise point where our theme acquires decisive significance, because the subject of the "fear of death" is indeed multi-faceted. Theologically, there is a great misunderstanding of this "fear," which is often transmitted through liturgical texts and homilies. On an existential—emotional—level, this fear is very real. At the same time, the Church propagates the incarnated love of God—which transfigures life—and thereby "beautifies" death liturgically through praise of Christ's Resurrection. How can one reconcile these two approaches?

This is the question I attempt to answer here by exploring the theological perspective of the fear of death. This fear is related to our inability to experience the existential meaning of death, very often due to trauma. Our most basic problem is not death itself, but rather an erroneous theological criterion (a false belief) that looks at death from an ethical and emotional point of view instead of as an ontological threat. This theme can be viewed from both a biological-cultural perspective and an ecclesial-resurrectional perspective. Let us consider both.

[2]Epicurus, *Fragment* 31.
[3]Gen 3.21.
[4]Rom 7.24.

Fear of Death as a Biological Fact

Death is deeply connected with our nature (i.e., with the mode of fallen nature), and it is no laughing matter. As the contemporary biologist William Clark observes:

> Human beings, uniquely among all living creatures on this earth, know that one day they will die. It is a painful knowledge. We have spent most of our history as a knowing species devising belief systems that help us either accept or deny that single fact. No human culture ignores it. It colors our experience as individuals, and often influences our collective actions. Death is a subject that simultaneously terrifies us and fascinates us. Understanding that terror and fascination is an important part of human psychology.[5]

Existence is permanently threatened by *death* (nothingness) and is constantly limited by it. Biology (in agreement, in this case, with patristic thought) assures us that, according to nature, every being is born as "dying," meaning that one begins to die biologically from the moment of conception and birth. The whole created world is dying while it exists and exists while it is dying; the life of the world and even our own lives do not embody "true life." Life as we know it is, in fact, a "process of being" on the ultimately straight path of the fall, permanently moving closer to and inevitably ending in death, which is genetically transmitted. The aphoristic idea that death is inherited through birth points us toward the realization that the death of every being begins with the initial death of just a few cells. This situation is perhaps what inspired a wise man to exclaim, "If you do not know how

[5]William R. Clark, *Sex and the Origins of Death* (Oxford: Oxford University Press, 1996), ix.

to die, don't worry; nature herself will teach you in the proper time; she will discharge that work for you; don't trouble yourself."[6]

If death is naturally existent even at the very inception of life, where does our fear of death come from? Is it, perhaps, natural to fear death? Is it natural to die? If it is, as many assert, why be afraid? How can we understand our nature, and is there something like a "fallen" nature? For the purpose of our discussion, let us agree to accept Adam as the first being in creation that God personally invited to become a god in communion with him, constituting him ontologically ("your creative command was the beginning and hypostasis of my being"),[7] and to thus transcend the death and corruption inherent in the nature of the world. His subsequent rejection of this invitation represents the "fall." After the "fall," all life within creation has a tendency to avoid death. Man especially bears the consequences because he is the only free *personal* being within creation. In every way, he tries desperately to avoid death, but he finally must give way and succumb to it. Wherein lies his failure? It is exactly in his continuous *battle to win life by avoiding death*. By doing this, he is affirming himself as a *self-determined* and *self-sufficient* entity. The more he attaches himself to life, especially to his individual life, the more it is confirmed that death is truly inevitable. It is not natural for a person or "ego" to consider life as an *object* to possess or grasp in order to forestall death. In trying to overcome death by loving and depending on himself and grasping hold of life, he is surviving by ignoring others whom he regards as potential enemies or rivals for his freedom, especially his freedom to live. This self-love, paradoxically, contains the very seed of corruption and death.

---

[6]A quotation attributed to Michel de Montaigne.

[7]St John of Damascus, from the Orthodox funeral service, tone 6 sticheron before the Beatitudes.

Fear of Death as a Theological Fact and "the Last Enemy"

There is an alternative to seeing man as simply a biological organism. Suspended between *eros* (ecstatic love) and *thanatos* (death), man can be measured not only by his biochemistry but also by his ecstatic freedom toward God. The world offers objectivity as a shelter, but, instead, it leads him to death, whereas *eros* for God is not easily quenched. Dealing with the world in an *individualistic* way causes man to direct this same *eros* toward the world, which eventually consumes man and leads to death. And from this comes our fear and anxiety. When our tissues and organs betray us and we begin to lose those things that make us human beings, how can one believe, preserve one's faith? "How [have] we [given] in to corruption, and bec[o]me partners with death?"[8]

Man is not simply a biological-mortal being (a "being-toward-death," in the Heideggerian sense), although mechanistic neurology and deterministic biochemistry can reduce us to a complex system of capacities and links that make us resemble a dying machine. Illnesses affect people, God's creations, but they do not tarnish the icon within nature. It is time to stop thinking of man as a "spiritual" being and start to see him as a *theo-bio-cultural* being. This means that we must allow for a transcendent impetus within man that enables him to overcome the fear of death and decide whether he will live in accordance with God or in accordance with his fallen nature. Whether healthy or ill, man is somehow inherently aware that the choice to live exclusively according to his fallen *nature* will destroy him at the end with the emotionless sway of *thanatos*. The same erotic power is able to "resurrect" him if he exercises his free will to live in accordance with

[8]St John of Damascus, from the Orthodox funeral service, tone 8 sticheron before the Beatitudes.

God by conquering his "self" and mortifying his selfish will. If this erotic power (desire for life) is not suffused with humility, it is deprived of grace and dies, generally after a period of panic, fear, and anxiety. Phenomenologically, man experiences a real conflict between biology, theology, and culture. In order to be fully whole, health must, therefore, be three-dimensional, or bio-theo-cultural.

The theological emphasis of the *bio-theo-cultural* concept of death was developed in the East under the influence of the Greek Church Fathers. In this theology, *thanatos*, or death, is seen as a personification of nothingness. However, in the Church Tradition, the notion of death was interpreted in a great variety of ways, often using images and metaphors. Some of the hymnographers tried to "contextualize" death, often euphemizing it, and give it a certain "meaning." But the Church never allowed death to entail any kind of "being" or existence (death has no being). St Paul considered death "the last enemy,"[9] because he spoke from an ontological perspective and through the prism of the Resurrection. Some of the later Fathers "softened" or even "beautified" death. From a non-resurrectional perspective, there are many interpretations, but Christians should never give up their Pauline indignation over death, in spite of its later neo-Platonic relativizations. Death is, according to Florovsky, a "painful metaphysical catastrophe."[10] As Elder Sophronios used to teach, "Death is not a 'friend' to be embraced."[11] It's also important to accept that the principal threat for a Christian is not the apocalyptic end of the world but gradual, cumulative decay and dying.

[9]Cf. 1 Cor 15.26.

[10]Georges Florovsky, *Creation and Redemption*, vol. 3 of *The Collected Works of Georgers Florovsky* (Belmont, MA: Nordland, 1976), 105.

[11]Elder Sophronios, *His Life is Mine*, trans. Rosemary Edmonds (Crestwood, NY: St Vladimir's Seminary Press, 1977), 34.

It should be inconceivable for the Church, with its dogma of the Resurrection, to neglect its beliefs concerning the unacceptability of death. Christians must not lose their indignation over death. Yet, the Church is a place of freedom and love that casts out every fear.

Fear of Death as Psychological-Religious Fact

The dominant concept of death in our Western culture, including even modern Orthodoxy, seems to presuppose the idea of life as an *individual possession*.

Is it not often said that "we all die alone"? It is from this perspective that we tend to speak about various fears of death: the fear of physical death; the "religious" fear of eternal separation from God; and, equally important, the fear of separation from our loved ones. In all these aspects, the focus is on an *individualistic* rather than a personalistic view of life, as we will describe later. So it seems only fitting to seek the roots of this fear in the reality of the "self."

This is precisely where some fundamental problems and questions about the self and the Church arise. Is the Church a religion? Is it here to meet man's individualistic (romantic, aesthetic, utopian) needs? Or does it represent the gathering at the banquet of life, where we partake of the food necessary for *true* existence, the Paschal mystery of Christ?

Religion per se cultivates the ability of an individual to set boundaries around oneself, thereby affirming one's self or "ego," and thus remaining in death. In the Church, on the contrary, "We know that we have passed out of death into life, because we love the brethren. He who does not love abides in death."[12] An ecclesial hypostasis (person) exercises his or her freedom in the ability to come forward in an

---

[12] 1 Jn 3.14.

ekstasis of the self, to overcome boundaries, to take part with others in community, and finally to confirm one's existence and one's own otherness *through someone else*, our brothers and sisters.

Fear of Death as Cultural (Contextual) Fact

The mindset and terminology of modernity is not well equipped for discussing death in a decisive way, as we, as Christians, wish to do. We must therefore escape from the category of the individual and enter into the realm of personhood.

There is also in our modern society a tendency to undervalue death, which is no doubt caused in part by society's ignorance of death. Against the fear of death our culture produces a set of logical arguments undervaluing both fear and death, reminiscent of how Epicurus dealt with the same topic: "Death, the most awful of evils, is nothing to us, since when we are, death is absent, and, when death is present, we are not any more. It is nothing, then, either to the living or to the dead."[13] A Serbian film director, Emir Kusturica, recently wrote a novel with the Huxleyan title *Death Is an Untested Rumor* [or *Hearsay*]. Steve Jobs once stated, "Death is a useful but purely intellectual concept." He also said:

> No one wants to die. Even people who want to go to heaven don't want to die to get there. And yet death is the destination we all share. No one has ever escaped it. And that is as it should be, because Death is very likely the single best invention of Life. It is Life's change agent. It clears out the old to make way for the new. Right now the new is you, but someday not too long from now,

[13]"Letter to Menoeceus," as translated in Robert Drew Hicks, *Stoic and Epicurean, Rpochs of Philosophy* (New York: Charles Scribner's Sons, 1910), 169.

you will gradually become the old and be cleared away. Sorry to be so dramatic, but it is quite true.[14]

The Response to the Fear of Death: The Christology of the Resurrection

In the end, the Resurrection is the only key to the problem of death, for only the Resurrection satisfies the thirst for eternity, removes the fear of death, and pacifies the longing to overcome corruption and death, which are innate to createdness. God did not come merely to participate in man's suffering but to abolish death, to destroy it.[15] In Christ's triumph over death, the annihilating touch of death is itself annihilated, vanquished in the instant that the Creator of Life descends to hell to burst its bonds. It is paradoxical, but true, that life has sprung up from the grave. The goal of the Incarnation is the abolishment of death and the eternal life of creation. There is no death where God reigns, and so there is no compromise between God and death. The ontology of love leading to communion justifies the centrality of the Resurrection in the economy of salvation.

There was no salvation from death for man and the creation without God himself intervening and taking upon himself the destiny of the world. The Lord, as the incarnate Love of God, took upon himself *our* death. The life that God gives us in Christ is the life that flows from the death of Christ himself; it is not an easy life and cannot be gained without *kenōsis* and the experience of death.

It is a common topic for the Fathers of the Church, who were concerned with these questions, that the root of the fear of death lies in the concept of man as an individual, because, for them, individualism is

[14]Steve Jobs's commencement address to graduating students at Stanford University on June 12, 2005.

[15]Cf. the church service of the Resurrection (Pascha).

intimately linked to death. From this perspective, Christians have only one "holy war" with the last enemy,[16] a sacred battle for their personal resurrection and the resurrection of their fellow human beings. Only this existential meaning of the Resurrection can change our perspective on death, for *by accepting death we demonstrate not only freedom but also love*, just as Christ "paradoxically convinced the lovers through death to pass to the Beloved one."[17]

How would we have been able to live in the midst of our sins if another had not mortified the body of our death—our sins—on the Cross? There is a great truth regarding this topic: for life to begin and to become our reality, death—at least for most—must precede. Only after passing through death do we acquire true life. As Fr John Behr points out:

> The Gospel of John is only read in Church during the Paschal season. Having gone through a lengthy period of preparation—the forty days of Lent and the weeks that lead up to Lent—we are tempted to feel that having reached Pascha, having duly examined ourselves and confessed ourselves as sinners, that we have arrived, that we have attained, somehow, the healing and salvation freely given to the paralytic, and that we can now have some time off, as it were, in which we can relax in the joy of Pascha. If this is what we think, then the Gospel today forces us to think again. Even having been freely granted salvation through Christ's Passion, we also, just as the healed paralytic, still have to strive to find Christ and to come to know who he is and what it is that he has done for us. It is not amongst the noise and disturbances of the crowd that we have the peace that we need to encounter Christ; rather

[16]Cf. 1 Cor 15.26.

[17]παραδόξως διὰ θανάτου πείθων τοὺς ἐραστὰς διαβῆναι πρὸς τὸν ποθούμενον (St Maximus the Confessor, *Epistle* 14).

Christ presents himself to the paralytic in the temple, for Christ has entered, through his Passion, into the inner shrine, a forerunner on our behalf, interceding for us as a high priest.[18]

This resurrectional experience poses several concrete consequences in the life of the Church. It has inspired the Church, for example, to develop its *baptismal* practice (the concept of baptism as a dying and resurrecting into Christ, a "putting on of Christ"), spiritual fatherhood (fathers who die for their children), monasticism (a "second baptism" and dying to the world), the eucharistic transfiguration of the world (which includes such matters as the overcoming of death—not only of spiritual death but also of *physical* death), and the insistence on the conversion of the human individual into a true person living in the image of the Holy Trinity.

Conclusions: *Fear of Death in the Ecclesial Experience*

In the mystery of the Eucharist, the Church preserves the only place where a personal *relationship* with any "other," even with a "deceased other," can be maintained and preserved, despite death's efforts to disrupt it. In the Church, we are taught that we exist because of the other's "benefactions seen and unseen,"[19] because others have sacrificed themselves for us, first among whom is the Lord himself. It is in this network of relationships that we admit that whatever true life we have and are able to receive is owed to the death or sacrifice of others. The Church is the locus where we willingly die in a Christ-like manner.

It should be evident that we are not comparing the Orthodox approach with other religious, philosophical, or medical perspectives.

---

[18]John Behr, *The Cross Stands while the World Turns: Homilies for the Cycles of the Year* (Crestwood, NY: St Vladimir's Seminary Press, 2014), 105.

[19]First prayer in the Anaphora of St John Chrysostom (after "It is truly meet").

Because the Church *is* the solution to the problem of death. *It* is the victory over death, and it has no intention of "taming" death. Sadly, contemporary Christians overlook the Church as the place of life where, with Christ and the grace of the Spirit, death is conquered and new life begins. As Fr Vasileios Gontikakis has noted, "After passing through death, all things have a different mode of existence."[20] How is this "new life" possible?

1. In the image of the crucified Christ who "takes away the sin of the world,"[21] the Church also receives the tragic and sinful experiences and failures of man, for it is the Body of the crucified Lord. In order to save the world, the Church must pass through the reality of death. As St Paul says, death takes place within "us" (the apostles), so that life can begin inside "you" (i.e., the Corinthians and other members of the Church).[22] This is what the *real* saints do. Without this identification with the tragic destiny of the world, there is no salvation of the world.

2. The great truth that modern treatments of death ignore is that fear of death is conquered only by taking upon oneself the death of others, so that they might live. To live truly means to die and then live. Those who are truly fearless in the face of death are those who die *daily* by sacrificing for others.[23] If they do not die, everlasting life cannot be born in their beloved ones (for example, in their spiritual children).

---

[20]Archimandrite Vasileios of Iveron, *The Thunderbolt of Ever-Living Fire* (Los Angeles: Sebastian Press, 2014), 52.

[21]Jn 1.29.

[22]Cf. 2 Cor 4.6–12.

[23]Cf. Elder Aimilianos, *The Way of the Spirit*, 116. Cf. St Athanasius, *The Life of St Antony* 19: "It is good for us to meditate on the Apostle's statement *I die daily* (1 Cor 15.31). If we too live our lives like this—as though we were going to die each day—we will not sin. I am saying this so that if we awaken each day and think: 'I will not be alive until evening,' and again when we are about to go to sleep, if we think, 'I am not going to wake up,' then we will not take for granted that our life is so certain when we know that it is measured out each day by Providence."

The Lord said, "Unless a grain of wheat falls into the earth and dies, it remains alone; but if it dies, it bears much fruit."[24] The logic of the Lord is completely paradoxical and leads to the final victory over every fear: "He who loves his life loses it, and he who hates his life in this world will keep it for eternal life."[25]

3. If we have anxiety over death, that means that we are seeking life without being willing to experience death first. In every generation, there were those who were ready to die for others, who loved others more than they loved themselves. Those who will sacrifice themselves for us are the only hope for us. The reason for this is that death can be vanquished only by something that is stronger than it—through love, which is "stronger than death."[26]

4. This is the mystery of the "power made perfect in weakness,"[27] but the weakness is not power per se. It is manifest as power only when man accepts his mortality as "leaven" for the grace of the Resurrection, as the field of the encounter between his freedom and the Love that brought us into being. The saints, exactly like Christ, took upon themselves the death of others so that these others might live. This is a reality that applies to all, especially those who have the gift of being a spiritual father.

5. The direction of life after the "fall," in fact, has always tended toward an individualism where each *individuum* attains its autonomy and self-sufficiency in the most negative way. To be a person in an individualistic way of life means to be independent and self-sufficient; it means that one isn't *interdependent* with others, except in matters of social or collective interests. This tragic state cannot be changed unless one dies as *individuum* and resurrects as a person through *the death of*

[24]Jn 12.24.
[25]Jn 12.25.
[26]Cf. Song 8.6.
[27]Cf. 2 Cor 12.9.

his or her selfishness. As Metropolitan John of Pergamon says in one of his (unpublished) homilies,

> Death conquers us, and we are not able to surpass it, because we try to surpass it by loving ourselves and putting all of our efforts into grasping hold of life, so that we survive by ignoring others. The reverse, then, is that which will give life to others. To efface your selfishness [i.e., the love for yourself] is a death. It is the *death of my self*. If I do not mortify my selfish self (which is equal to my death), I will not be able to exist; for the other to exist presupposes the death of ourselves for the other.[28]

6. We must understand, however, that mortification of our self via asceticism without *love* can be demonic, because love demands *ekstasis,* freedom from the demands of fallen existence. St John the Theologian exclaims, "We know that we have passed out of death into life, because we love the brethren. He who does not love abides in death."[29] So we arrive at the crucial point where only true love can unmask the taboos and camouflages of nature, crisscrossed with malevolent, threatening, uncontrollable forces. Unless our death comes from love for the other, it does not fulfill its destiny.

7. In the language of the Church, "to live" means to be ἑτοιμοθάνατος (ready to die), or rather "just born" and "ready to die." When we are ready to say to ourselves, "we are to blame," it means that we are ready to mortify our selfish will and take upon ourselves the death of the other.

8. It is only in this way that we can understand the Lord's words: "It is to your advantage that I go away, for if I do not go away, the Counselor will not come to you."[30] Likewise, and paradoxically, if our loved

[28]Metropolitan John of Pergamon, Homily on July 12, 2007.
[29]1 Jn 3.14.
[30]Jn 16.7.

ones are not separated from us, we will not find true comfort. If we do not leave others, they will not be comforted. This is the mystery of our humble "non-appearance,"[31] which is advantageous, both for our freedom and for the freedom of our beloved ones: so that it can be tested, tempted, and proved. That is the "freedom of absence" that only the Holy Spirit, the Spirit of communion, bestows on those who love.

Thus far we have highlighted what we might call the "ascetic" aspect of the fear of death, i.e., the struggle of man to liberate himself from "self-referentiality" through his relationships with others. But, through his relationships, man also emerges as a eucharistic being, who sees other members as unique, unrepeatable, and irreplaceable persons. A Eucharist that offers only "forgiveness of sins" and not also "life eternal" is not an Orthodox Eucharist.

It is out of the eucharistic perspective that St John the Theologian proclaims, "He who does not love abides in death."[32] Sanctity cannot exist outside of the "other" because the other serves as the terminal or reference of holiness. The "other," at the same time, is also the cause of my holiness and not a threat to it. By cultivating such an ethos of free love inside ourselves, we also become prepared, at least to some degree, to die so that others may live: "I told you that I am he; so, if you seek me, let these men go."[33]

Only a person who confesses the words "For me, your creative command is both cause and hypostasis"[34] (ἀρχή μοι καὶ ὑπόστασις) has overcome the fear of death. That person has buried the seed of his or her existence, and from it has grown a joy able to conquer death.

[31]See Mt 13.31–32.
[32]1 Jn 3.14.
[33]Jn 18.8.
[34]St John of Damascus, from the Orthodox funeral service, tone 6 sticheron before the Beatitudes.

PART II

Uniqueness, Gender, and Self

How Can We Be
Holy and Unique?

> Pray you never learn just how good it can be to see
> another face; I hadn't a lot of hope to begin with, but
> after so long I had none.
> —Dr Mann, *Interstellar*, directed by Christopher Nolan

ONE DAY, somewhere in the desert near the Nile, not far from Troe, when the brethren were conversing about love, Abba Joseph quoted Abba Agathon, who had said, "If it were possible for me to find a leper, to give him my body and take on his, I would do it gladly; for that is perfect love,"[1] and, one might add, perfect holiness. This exchange illustrates particularly well the relation between the two notions we are contemplating here.

The idea of the holiness of a person is deeply rooted in biblical faith, especially in the Christian Church. In view of this, God is called and experienced as the personal and Holy Being[2] *par excellence*. Bearing in mind that man was created "in the image" of the *holy* God, it is not surprising that the Church has a well-developed sensitivity for the holiness of the *human* person.

---

[1]Abba Agathon, Saying 26, in *Give Me a Word: The Alphabetical Sayings of the Desert Fathers*, trans. John Wortley, Popular Patristics Series 52 (Yonkers, NY: St Vladimir's Seminary Press, 2014), 58.

[2]In 1 Sam 6.20, *God* is identified as *Holy* within the same context.

What exactly would "You shall be holy, for I am holy"[3] mean if we were to examine it within its original context, detached from subsequent notions of *holiness*? Namely, apart from the ethical meaning (which is emphasized in the biblical tradition), can the notion of holiness also contain a personalistic meaning (which is implied)? Let us examine these theological questions in order to ascertain their effect on anthropology and ecclesiology.

The Biblical Concept of Holiness

The Semitic word *qadosh* or *godesh* is translated in the Septuagint as "saint," ἅγιος (*holy*). It actually means to cut, to separate (to be independent), to radically differentiate, to clean.[4] It follows that holy is he who is separate from the rest (which definitely applies to God); a holy person is someone who is different and independent from other people, and holy are those things that are separate from the rest.[5] This is the etymological concept of holy. Etymology without theology, however, leaves us with an incomplete explanation. Therefore, let us see what light theology sheds on the subject.

The biblical approach to the idea of holiness exceeds the psychological meaning of holiness held by the ancient Greeks: that is, dread, fear, being in awe of a higher power or its bearer.[6] To put it simply, the Bible, by offering an ontology of love, transcends the concepts of holiness as an expression of ethical individualism and a *mysterium fascinandum et tremendum*[7] and leads us—when the concept of holiness is

[3] 1 Pet 1.16; Lev 11.44–45.

[4] The subject of purity and purification is the dominant theme in Leviticus 17–26, especially in the "code of holiness."

[5] Wis 6.10: "For those who keep the holy precepts hallowed shall be found holy."

[6] See *Theological Dictionary of the New Testament*, ed. Gerhard Kittel and Gerhard Friedrich (Grand Rapids, MI: Eerdmans, 1985), 14–17.

[7] The expression originates with Rudolf Otto's *The Idea of the Holy* (Oxford: Oxford University Press, 1923).

connected with absolute *otherness* (God's otherness)—to the absolute Other. It is not difficult to see, then, how the Bible identified the Holy One with God, who is the Trinity. In his absolute transcendence in relation to the cosmos, Yahweh alone is the Holy One, in his Trinitarian, perfect, and unique way. Hence, holiness is no longer an abstract notion.

In order to express this faith with a particular emphasis on the uniqueness of God's holiness in the Old Testament, God is called holy three times: "Holy, Holy, Holy is the Lord of Hosts."[8] The Church has valued this moment *liturgically* in its eucharistic anaphora (both in the East and in the West's *Sanctus*) and *canonically* (eucharistic reconciliation with others was the objective of the Church councils). From this same perspective, the Church Fathers interpreted Isaiah's threefold "Holy" as Trinitarian, not because of a narrow "dogmatic" interpretation, but rather because of a hypostatic-existentialistic one. In view of this, holiness should not be understood as one of the qualities of the *nature* of God, but as the fundamental characteristic of the Triune *Persons*—the unique, unrepeatable, and personal Hypostases. When God, the only Holy One and the only Truth, *invites* us to holiness according to a *life in Truth*, this invitation extends to a manner of existence that is appropriate only to him. This is the most perfect invitation, which nothing can surpass, either in this or in the next world, because it enables every participant to acquire a true hypostatic existence.

So, the correct *theological* context of holiness is biblical—that is, it pertains to the Old and New Testaments. "You shall be holy, for I am holy"[9] is an invitation extended to the community as well, not only to the individual. This is very significant. For the aim of all creation is God the Logos' arrival in history, in order to recapitulate not only man

---

[8] Is 6.3.
[9] 1 Pet 1.16; Lev 11.44–45.

but also all of creation in the Person of God the Son and thus to unite
them with the only Holy One. Both man and all of creation seek none
other than this Holy God, who is coming. Otherwise, it would mean
that God created the world without intending for it to have a *hypostatic*
union with him. The Father's holiness, which Christ as High Priest
invokes in his prayer,[10] is the foundation of his request for all the faithful to remain in communion with him.[11] No one has ever reached perfection without a personal relationship with the *Holy One*, that is, with
the Absolute Other. Hence, man's first *fall* can be explained within this
context. Adam's rejection of God meant a rejection of holiness, which
properly understood is, of course, constitutive of existence, or otherness, which is not merely some quality. In his aspiration to become a
god on his own (that is, without the Other), Adam rejected the Holy
One as the constituent of his existence and proclaimed himself as the
final explanation of his own existence. In his "fallen" existence, holiness and communion cannot coincide with each other at all, as they
do in the case of the divine, Triune existence.

So, the central question seems to be: "Who shall be able to come
before this holy Lord?"[12] since Adam, the first man, could not manage
to do it. Because the biblical God is completely extraordinary, how
can the ontological abyss between God and the world be overcome? St
Maximus the Confessor's (seventh-century) answer to this question is
that this divide can be bridged through the hypostatic union, that is,
through the Hypostasis of the Son. God does not overcome the abyss
through nature or through some energy of his own but through the
adaptation of his *tropos*, through his way of existence. Herein lies the

[10]Jn 17.11.
[11]Cf. W. Pannenberg, *Systematic Theology*, vol. 1 (Edinburgh: T&T Clark, 1991),
399.
[12]1 Sam 6.20.

mystery of Christ.[13] In this way, God's relationship with the world is not based on an ethical, psychological, or religious dimension, but on an *ontological* one. Man achieves his complete realization only through hypostatic communion with God in Christ. Holiness stems only from him and from a relationship with him. Thus, he who enters into communion with God can become exceptional and unique, because God is the One who is completely and radically unique, or "completely other" (*ganz andere*).

Now we arrive at the crux of our discussion. Does being exceptional, which *qadosh* implies, entail separation? Let us examine this idea, which at first glance implies a transcendental dimension and in its final analysis identifies holiness with uniqueness. The Bible insists on the holiness of God precisely because he is special, *separate*, and therefore something *completely different* from everything else. Bishop Atanasije Jevtić[14] sees a radical gap in the notion of holiness between the classical Greco-Roman and Eastern traditions on the one hand, and the Hebrew-biblical tradition on the other. Plato's idea of God as the supreme Good is the highest and best link in the chain of beings; however, it remains only a link because it is not the personal God. Evidently, the biblical *qadosh* (holy) means something entirely different, in regard to cosmology as well.

Why, then, is holiness as a *mysterium fascinandum et tremendum* (Rudolf Otto) an inadequate way to express the encounter between holy God and man? First of all, this is because of the *separation* that remains the basic characteristic of this relation. The biblical God, by contrast, paradoxically moves toward creation through *eros* and love (ecstasy), respecting the holiness of the world.[15] The biblical approach

---

[13]*Amb.* 5 (PG 91:1056) and *Amb.* 41 (PG 91:1308C and 1313).

[14]"On Holiness and Responsibility," in *The Living Tradition in the Church* [in Serbian] (Trebinje: V. Banja, 1998), 378–80.

[15]"God moves in such a way that He instills an *inner relationship* (σχέσιν

points to God as *holy*, because he freely reveals himself as a loving Being and invites us to an encounter with him, to the experience of a relation.[16] His appearance to Elijah on the mountain was not manifested in lightning and thunder (which indeed would have caused fascination and trembling) but in the "sound of a gentle breeze."[17] This encounter with the holy God has almost nothing in common with the "natural" idea of a God who arouses fascination and trembling.[18] The relation with the only Holy One, Christ, is a loving relation, completely and infinitely intimate, a personal-holistic encounter, precisely because Christ is a personal and relational Being *par excellence*. Therefore, the dimension of holiness that the natural religions lack can be termed *hypostatic*. This dimension complements that part of holiness characterized as "ecstatic," which is man's stepping forward in order to encounter the Holy One.

In the Church, each saint differs from the others in his or her absolute otherness, an otherness that is unique, irreproducible, and irreplaceable. Anything that violates or undermines the absolute uniqueness of a person changes it into a means toward an end. There is nothing holier than the person as an absolute otherness and uniqueness. Let us illustrate this through a number of historical examples.

Some Historical Examples

What happens when we continue this logic and ask ourselves whether holiness is attainable only by being distinct and separate? This is a key question, but we have already discovered in the discussion above that

ἐνδιάθετον) of eros and love in those who are able to receive it. He moves naturally, attracting the desire of those to Him who are turned toward him" (PG 91:1260C).

[16]1 Jn 4.19: "We love, because he first loved us."

[17]1 Kg 19.12.

[18]St Augustine conveys a similar experience in *Confessions* 9.9.

the answer is no; the context of the Testament (or Covenant) alone excludes such a possibility. To be exact, for both theology and the Church, a holy man is he who is distinct and unique, and furthermore one who has attained *the uniqueness of a person from the anonymity of an individual.* Since, however, a person does not exist for himself or herself alone—and here is the quintessence of hagiology—the realization of his or her authentic self occurs through the communion of persons, that is, through *communio sanctorum.* This is the reason why Church Tradition teaches that each saint is unique and distinct as a result of a unique and irreproducible relationship he or she has attained with the unique and irreproducible Holy One within the liturgical (common) experience of the Church. Here, it is important to emphasize the context within which the call "You shall be holy"[19] requires one to love one's neighbor as oneself ("You shall love your neighbor as yourself; I am the Lord"[20]).

Therefore, in view of the ethical and personal dimension of holiness, we can assert that the objective of every human being is not moral perfection *through* holiness, but rather *uniqueness,* that is, an otherness, which is manifested in communion with others. It should be pointed out that otherness and distinction—that is, just being different—are not one and the same thing. Distinctiveness can be expressed in terms of qualities (which everyone can have) but does not apply to otherness (because personal otherness and uniqueness exclude that).[21] After all, the Church, in the Divine Liturgy, commemorates[22] *individual* saints

[19]Lev 19.1.

[20]Lev 19.18.

[21]This is the reason why some theologians are in favor of introducing so-called "ethical apophatism" in the realm of culture. For more detailed information, see John Zizioulas, "On Being a Person: Towards an Ontology of Personhood," in *Persons, Divine and Human,* ed. Christoph Schwoebel and Colin Gunton (New York: T&T Clark, 1991), 33–46.

[22]One should keep in mind that here the most accurate meaning of holiness is

and rarely saints as a general category. They are commemorated by their respective calendar dates and names: every individual ascetic and martyr. Only as such, that is, as unique and irreproducible, can they serve as inexhaustible sources of inspiration to Christians. Consider, for example, Abba Sisoe's attitude toward death, Abba Anthony's sober vigilance before the mystery of God's judgments, the holy Martyr Polycarp in his ecstatic passion during martyrdom for Christ, and the challenges of St Simeon the Fool for Christ. They are all permanent and eternal examples of a sacrificial love "stronger than death." At the same time, they pose an existential challenge to man. Perhaps a maximalistic anthropology (an expectation of a high ideal from man) stems from their hagiography, which at first glance seems unattainable for modern man and difficult for those who are used to a leisurely lifestyle. However, this kind of anthropology causes an awakening from a dogmatic—and also probably from an ethical—"slumber." The martyrs who offered themselves wholly to God serve as an example. Their being was united with God to such an extent that one can no longer speak of any *separation* between them, although *distinction* (i.e., otherness) certainly continues to exist and remains forever. The saints of the Church are those persons (the Theotokos, the apostles, the martyrs, and ascetics) who, in one way or another, have overcome the anonymity of nature in their own and irreproducible manner and have united themselves with Christ, the "only Holy One," in a personal and unique way.

by way of liturgical remembrance. Namely, ontologically a saint is remembered only *liturgically*, in a union that reveals permanence (eternity, intransience) here and now, and not psychologically through the function of memory, but by the remembrance of God the Father through his Son in the Holy Spirit.

The Church as the Space for Holiness and Uniqueness

How does the theology of holiness illustrated thus far find its realization within the Church? Church Tradition cherishes the eucharistic approach according to which we accept the other as other and different, apart from all other qualifications, such as sinfulness, morality, sex, age, and so on. Contrary to Jean-Paul Sartre's idea that "Hell is other people,"[23] the saint, according to patristic thought, always needs the *Other* and the *other*. It is precisely this type of logic that makes Orthodoxy so valuable to all those who lately are in favor of otherness and differences. So, how is otherness experienced in the Orthodox Church?

In patristics, we hear about relational and not objective holiness.[24] The "other" is a *conditio sine qua non* of holiness, rather than a "given fact." The Desert Fathers, who lived apart from the "world," were nevertheless equally dependent on the other as their brother. There is no greater principle on this subject than the one expressed by St John the Theologian: "He who loves God should love his brother also,"[25] and "We know that we have passed out of death into life, because we love the brethren. He who does not love abides in death."[26] Sanctity cannot exist outside of the other, because the other serves as the terminal or reference of holiness. The other is also the cause of my holiness, at the same time, understood in a dynamic sense as movement. St Maximus says that the members of the Church "run together according to their common aim and purpose, each man advancing equally well

[23]Jean-Paul Sartre, *No Exit and Three Other Plays* (New York: Vintage Books, 1955).

[24]The idea of venerating icons in *relational* terms, which was developed by theologians St (John Damascene, St Theodore the Studite, and others), is closely connected to the idea of "relational sainthood."

[25]1 Jn 4.21.

[26]1 Jn 3.14.

in accordance with the good that is proper to him."[27] The ultimate destination of this movement of holiness is the only Holy One *par excellence*, who affirms each individual "saint" and in whom every individual saint finds his or her ontological foundation.

The Apostle Paul stresses that a union (here he refers to the eucharistic communion) must affirm and sanctify not only the totality and entirety but also the *otherness* of its members. This is the reason why St Paul calls all Christians *holy*.[28] We have already mentioned that *qadosh* refers to uniqueness or exceptionality. It is precisely in the Church that this uniqueness or otherness (difference) ceases to be a division, something negative, but becomes something positive, good, and, at the same time, indispensable—that is, a prerequisite. The personal charismata of holiness in the Church are so varied that no member can say to another one, "I have no need of you."[29] The diversity of the saints and their otherness are affirmed in the Eucharist. In Christianity, this means that *when we respect someone's holiness, we actually respect his otherness and vice versa*. Whenever this principle is not applied, the meaning of holiness is violated.

So, holiness that in any way excludes those placed in a second category—whether by race, sex, age, or profession—is *opposed* to holiness. Holiness that harbors a preference for monastic-ascetics, children, or black or white saints also defies holiness. The Church must include all of them in its Eucharist because this is the only way of overcoming the differences of nature and society.[30]

It is interesting that this matter accurately expresses the necessary balance between the Body of Christ and the communion of the Holy

---

[27] *Amb.* 57, Constas II, 255 (PG 91:1381A).
[28] See 1 and 2 Corinthians, Galatians, 1 and 2 Thessalonians, etc.
[29] 1 Cor 12.21.
[30] Cf. Zizioulas, *Communion and Otherness*, 8.

Spirit in ecclesiology.[31] Encroachments result in an increase of individuality, elitism, and various divisions—a tendency present in the Church throughout its history. Central to this idea is the notion that, historically, the Holy Spirit is especially "concerned" with the inspiration of "worthy" individuals. As Stavros Yangazoglou observes,

> By regarding the Church as a sanatorium for souls and not as the body of the Christ of both history and eschatological expectation, we turn her into a community of charismatics, precisely because she has spirit-bearing saints in her body as an elite. The conclusion of this is that the Church is holy, not because of Christ, the holy head of her body, but because of the charismatic saints.[32]

Indeed, there is a misconception that certain "spirit-filled" saints with special charismata (usually of the monastic order) exist who "are the preservers of the truth" in contrast to the "rest" of the Church, the episcopacy, the clergy, and the people.

Implications

So far, we have seen how holiness as an ethical concept arrives at holiness as a personalistic concept. Still, there is one more thing that must be emphasized: If we understand holiness exclusively as a category of *nature* (an attribute of God's nature, as in dogmatic textbooks), instead of as a *hypostatic* otherness, it will appear as a mystery that arouses fascination and trembling, a mystery that remains forever *separate* and *out of reach* for us, precisely because it does not have an ontology of love that "casts out fear."[33] If, however, we understand holiness as part

---

[31]More about this in Stavros Yangazoglou, "Eucharistic Ecclesiology and Monastic Spirituality in Modern Orthodox Theology," *St Vladimir's Theological Quarterly* 61 (2017): 373–94.

[32]Yangazoglou, "Eucharistic Ecclesiology," 382.

[33]1 Jn 4.18.

of a *hypostasis*, we will not experience this separation—this distance—
but rather a *surprise*: the encounter of the hypostases of God and men,
detached *by nature*, but united in love, wherein "perfect love" truly
"casts out fear." In this union, man's holiness is manifested as a unique
and personal otherness, as a gift from the only Holy One (the Other)
and not as a trait of nature.

Finally, let us say something about the idea of *relational holiness*.
Every individual manifestation of holiness of the Christian person in
the entire existence and life of the Church points to the only Holy
One, Jesus Christ. The iconographic principle of *relational reverence*
(σχετικὴ προσκύνησις, relational, conditional reverence, dependent on
the prototype) is completely applicable to the reality of holiness. Thus,
any holiness without a reference to the holiness of God and the Church
would be an oxymoron, that is, a "demonic" holiness and a *contradictio
in adiecto*. The "fall" is an attempt to attain one's own holiness, with
the individual's self as the point of reference, which is the reason why
it leads to death. Therefore, every saint, out of humility, consciously
and deliberately "transfers" and directs holiness to the prototype of
holiness, Christ—that is, he or she lets it "ascend to the prototype."[34] In
short, in the experience of the Church, *holiness* represents the immediate grace-filled reality of an existential and mystagogical nature, which
is experienced here and now only in part, as an "icon," but will be fully
and perfectly experienced in the future timeless Kingdom of God.

[34]St Basil the Great, *On the Holy Spirit* 18.45 (PG 32:149C).

Does Gender Have a Future?

> Sex makes everything more complicated. Even not having
> it, because the not having it . . . makes it complicated.
> —Amanda, *The Holiday*, directed by Nancy Meyers

THE IDEAL OF ASCETICISM (and a sign of perfection), inspired and reflected in the Gospel, is to not divide people on the basis of sexual orientation and gender identity. The story of the monk who on a certain journey met desert-dwelling nuns is very indicative. Seeing them, he left the road and gave them a wide berth. The abbess invited him over to herself and reproached him with the following words: "If you were a perfect monk, you would not have seen us as women."[1]

The specter of gender is one of the most persistent cultural problems. Many have entered into an alliance to exorcise this specter: conservative politicians, some clergy, radical intellectuals, and moralists of all kinds and fashions. On the other side, almost in the same number, are those who have embraced it, fashioning a romantic "gender identity," even a "theology of gender." Clearly, this problem is partly due to the existing confusion between the concepts of sex (which is biologically based) and gender (which is psychosocially based). What would be an Orthodox approach to this problem?

Male and female cannot easily be reconciled. Are they not mutually inclusive and exclusive at the same time? Is it not true that the male, by

---

[1] Cf. Susanna Elm, *"Virgins of God": The Making of Asceticism in Late Antiquity* (Oxford: Clarendon Press, 1994), 267.

definition, is the opposite sex/gender[2] of the female (and vice versa) and that their relationship is *so problematic* that it is closely linked with the "ancestral sin" of the biblical account? One could say that the fall (the original problem between man and God and between and among humans) leads to a gender identity crisis and to an obvious *rupture* between the genders.

How does theology look upon gender, on the otherness of gender, and, consequently, on gender-based relations? That this rupture between the sexes seems to have driven human history from the very beginning indicates that it is a part of man's *natural* state.[3] Yannaras remarks that "nature is skillful in the tricks she plays with the unconscious. She plays the game of self-interest even with the mode of virtue."[4] It would take an entire volume to describe this reality, a reality to which our culture subscribes in many ways. Biology and nature also confirm that this is a *universal*, almost pathological, problem.[5] Almost everything that exists, whether consciously, unconsciously, or even nonconsciously, undergoes and "suffers" this discord.[6] It is now widely accepted not merely that men and women (and also boys and

[2]The word for this in Slavonic, "*pol*," implies an inevitable attraction, almost a magnetic one, like "polarity" in chemistry.

[3]We will discuss sexuality as a *social* construction later. "Because sexuality is a social construction, individuals as individuals are not free to experience *eros* just as they choose. Yet just as the extraction and appropriation of surplus value by the capitalist represents a choice available, if not to individuals, to society as a whole, so too sexuality and the forms taken by eros must be seen as at some level open to change" (N. Hartsock, *Money, Sex and Power* [Boston: Northeastern University Press, 1985], 178).

[4]Christos Yannaras, *Variations on the Song of Songs* (Brookline, MA: Holy Cross Orthodox Press, 2005), 125.

[5]See below our further consideration of the connection between nature, death, sex, and sexual reproduction, based on Zizioulas and the modern biologist Clark (*Sex and the Origins of Death*), in Zizioulas, "On Being Other," in *Communion and Otherness*, 58–61.

[6]Cf. Zizioulas's remarks in "On Being Other," in *Communion and Otherness*, 57.

girls, and even animals) are programmed to behave differently[7] from one another, but also that the sexual *division* (not only difference[8]) is part of the very foundation of our civilization. All of nature acts in such a way that these distinctions become dialectically opposed. Academics still debate which of the differences between the sexes are "biological"[9]—in the sense that they have been honed by evolution— and which are "cultural" or "environmental" and might more easily be altered by changed circumstances.[10]

Questioning the Ontology of Gender

In an attempt to provide a critical analysis of the otherness of gender from the ontological perspective of Eastern Orthodox theology, we here endeavor to present the ecclesial and patristic standpoint on the theological perspective on gender (i.e., culturally and historically based differences in the roles, attitudes, and behaviors of men and

[7]When boys and girls are born, they are already different, and they favor different toys from the beginning ("The Mismeasure of Woman," *Economist*, August 3, 2006).

[8]Here we intentionally say "division" and not "difference" because the latter is blessed, while the former is pathological. Zizioulas finds the most analytical articulation of this view in St Maximus the Confessor (see below).

[9]For example, men and women seem to perceive pain in different ways; "that may mean they sometimes need different pain-relief drugs" ("Sex and Drugs," *Economist*, July 21, 2005).

[10]See, for example, Georgia Warnke, *Debating Sex and Gender* (Oxford: Oxford University Press, 2011). Biological explanations of human behavior are making a comeback as the generation of academics who feared them as a covert way of justifying eugenics, or of thwarting Marxist utopianism, retire. The success of neo-Darwinism has provided an intellectual underpinning for the discussion about *why some differences between the sexes might be innate*. And new scanning techniques have enabled researchers to examine the brain's interior as it works, showing that male and female brains do, at one level, operate differently. The results, however, do not always support past clichés about what the differences in question actually are.

women), which is a greatly important, yet neglected, subject within Orthodox theology. This study traces the relationship between communion and otherness, questioning the ontology of gender and sex. The starting points are the biblical references to God's creation of man and *attaching* him to the other gender, then *detaching* him from gender (as a condition *sine qua non* for the Kingdom, i.e., the eschaton), and finally *reattaching* (recapitulation) *all* in Christ[11] as the Other *par excellence*. The ontology of communion and otherness[12] is at the center of the theological project of Metropolitan John Zizioulas, and here we will explore aspects of his theology that should be more influential in the modern theological discussion about gender and, furthermore, where his work could fruitfully complete the contributions of other theologians. Zizioulas, arguably the most influential Orthodox theologian of the past and current century, has transfused the implications of patristic theology into contemporary theology more than any other modern theologian. He has the great gift of very clearly summarizing various patristic theories and academic studies into a single, holistic perspective.

We'll also discuss this subject with regard to the testimony of the contemporary Christian Church in our postmodern world.[13] Like the

[11]Cf. "In the beginning He made them male and female . . . For this reason a man shall leave his father and mother and be *joined to his wife*: and the two shall become one flesh" (Mt 19.5); as opposed to the Christological perspective: "And every one who has *left* . . . [his] *wife* . . . for my name's sake, will receive a hundredfold, [and] *inherit eternal life*" (cf. Mt 19.29; Mk 10.29–30; Lk 14–26; 18.29–30); "And Jesus said to them, 'The sons *of this age* marry and are given in marriage; but those who are accounted worthy to attain to that age and to the resurrection from the dead neither marry nor are given in marriage, for they cannot die any more, because they are equal to angels and are sons of God, being sons of the resurrection'" (Lk 20.34–36).

[12]He develops it in many of his studies, but most analytically in his book *Communion and Otherness*.

[13]See, for example, John Zizioulas, Ὀρθοδοξία καὶ σύγχρονος κόσμος [Orthodoxy and the Modern World] (Nicosia, 2006).

Church Fathers, especially the Cappadocians, the goal of modern theology should be to interpret the Gospel existentially and contextually by entering into a deep dialogue with the surrounding culture and the philosophy of science. A modern theologian should never write without considering the implication of his or her words for modern man. *Theology* is that much more precious when we consider that it is the only decisive means of dealing with the problem of gender, because the arguments of Tradition alone do not sufficiently address it.[14]

Let's Not Sexualize It!

There is no doubt that the current problem between the genders is a direct result of what, in theological language, we call the "fall of man." No matter how we understand the "fall," since the first humans (Adam and Eve), an abnormality has been built into the very roots of our existence and inherited through our birth. This is the fear of the "opposite other." And this fear has become second nature. Cultural stereotyping is an unlikely explanation for this entire universal "abnormality." John Zizioulas argues that this is a result of the first man's rejection of the Other *par excellence*: our Creator. The essence of the first-created couple's "ancestral sin" is fear of the Other,[15] which is part of the rejection of God. Once the affirmation of the "self" ("*you* will be like *God*" from Genesis 3.3) is realized through the rejection of the Other (rejection of *ekstasis* and submission to the dictates of nature)—what Adam, in his freedom, chose to do—it is only natural for the other to become an enemy and a threat. A theological and existential consequence of this

---

[14]Zizioulas characteristically notes, "Past positions of the Church, which were based upon the society and culture of the time, cannot simply be transferred to all societies and cultures of other time periods, dissociated from their respective theological context" (*Orthodoxy and the Modern World*, 37).

[15]Zizioulas, *Communion and Otherness*, 1–2.

is that *reconciliation* with God is a necessary precondition for reconciliation with any "other,"[16] gender otherness included.

The opposition and bipolarity (and not simply differences or distinctions) between masculinity and femininity, since it is a problem
of our *nature*, has naturally become part of our culture: differences
between the sexes are so often popularized and played up in the popular media that people tend to pay them disproportionate attention. All
this implies that our culture cultivates a taboo vis-à-vis the opposite
gender—with all the attendant attraction and hidden charms, as well.
This taboo says that no human being is dispassionate or disinterested
with regard to the gender opposite of his own (although homosexuals
deny this). We feel more and more dependent on the presence of the
opposite sex. At the same time, we are forced and even encouraged
to consider the opposite sex more as a *temptation* than as a *blessing*
(a friend or fellow man). In the film *Collateral Beauty*,[17] Whit asks
Amy if he can kiss her, and she responds, "Let's not sexualize it." An
identity constructed on gender identity proves problematic. And it will
continue to be challenging, because it does not lead to a *free* relational
mode of existence and an identity free from the dictates of nature.

What is the problem with nature? As the modern theologian Christos Yannaras observes:

> Our human nature plays a game of self-interest with the mode
> of life, pursuing the mode of life in the delusion of love. There
> is no love which does not pass through phases of sacrificial self-
> denial and total self-offering. In fact, phases of life become nature's
> weapon for winning the other, for possessing him, for making
> him our own. With these weapons nature defends its interests,

[16]Ibid.

[17]*Collateral Beauty,* directed by David Franke (Burbank, CA: New Line Cinema,
2016), film.

prepares positions for attack, when the other begins to reveal himself through his own natural needs and independent desires.[18]

But is it correct to say that gender relationships do not lead to a free relational ontology? Why is the transcendence of gender identity's exclusiveness necessary? Zizioulas, for one, doesn't seem willing to rephrase his observations "on the other" in order to formulate the relationship between the genders, male-female. But, why?

Interaction with the (opposite) gender is *natural* (i.e., based on nature, not person) as well as "mechanical." There is nothing more *natural*, and thus inevitable, than to desire the *other* based on gender identity.[19] It would be *unnatural* to avoid this interaction; *almost* all[20] animals, humans included, are *not* hypocritical either in or with their

[18]Yannaras, *Variations*, 14.

[19]See below our further elaboration of this.

[20]Certainly, there exist in nature examples of sexually *indifferent* beings (so-called single-celled microorganisms and, indeed, some people) but this does not deny the general principle. Asexual reproduction is not, however, limited to single-celled organisms. Sexual reproduction typically requires the involvement of two individuals or gametes, one from each opposite type of sex. On the other hand, some of the species that are capable of reproducing asexually, like hydra, yeast, and jellyfish, may also reproduce sexually. The existence of life without reproduction was the subject of some speculation until recently when C. Venter and H. Smith, the two American biologists, made a bacterium that has an artificial genome—creating a living creature with no ancestor. This will be a real challenge for theology: the possibility—through synthetic biology—of creating new, useful organisms. Evolution by artificial selection is likely to prove almost as wasteful as the kind by natural selection (there are those that worry about the proliferation of gene synthesis). But almost all technologies can be used for ill as well as good. The ability to make genomes, coupled to a far greater understanding of how they lead to the structures of complex organisms, could one day allow simulacra of such creatures to be made by synthetic biology. In any case, though dinosaurs have left no usable DNA, other more recently departed creatures have been more generous. Imagine, e.g., allying synthetic biology with the genome of Neanderthal man and comparing this with the DNA of modern humans, in the hope of finding the essential differences between the two (See "Genesis Redux," *Economist*, March 20, 2010). But will someone dare to create a Neanderthal and ask him?

sexuality (this is valid even for homosexual relationships, for reasons that will be discussed elsewhere). They are *biologically* concerned with and apprehensive about sex. Temptations (dangers or challenges) are implicit in the presence of the (opposite) sex, but there is nothing more natural than to exercise sexuality, since the other—either he or she—is useful for both the biological and social happiness of the individual. "From a generalized biological perspective (one which applies to all mammals), an individual of the opposite sex becomes an object of the sex drive to the degree which the individual is offered for the attainment of pleasure."[21]

However, it is not possible to have an ontology of sexuality for two reasons. First, it is a *natural* fact that does not allow a *relational* otherness to survive as ever-being (ἀεὶ εἶναι). And second, it does not belong to the eschatological state of being.[22] This is consistent with Zizioulas's main axiom: "Only that which survives at the end possesses true being."[23]

A Wild Cat of Insatiable Appetite

As we suggested earlier, the essential "sin" of gender consists in its incapacity to overcome the inherent natural law present in it, which is primarily oriented toward maximizing reproduction. Every aspect of the male-female relationship is a result of given biological laws. Every particular gender coming into existence is *tuned* "to bring about other

[21]Christos Yannaras, *Relational Ontology* (Brookline, MA: Holy Cross Orthodox Press, 2011), 24.

[22]See Mt 22.30. Also: "The sons of *this age* marry and are given in marriage; but those who are accounted worthy to attain to *that age* and to the resurrection from the dead neither marry nor are given in marriage, for *they cannot die any more*, because they are equal to angels and are sons of God, being *sons of the resurrection*" (Lk 20.34–36).

[23]Zizioulas, "On Being Other," in *Communion and Otherness*, 68n156.

particularities which would secure the survival of the species."[24] This mechanism is tied up with the process of death, as modern biology confirms today.[25] This leads us to conclude that there is a deficient ontology present in gender. Subsequently, every form of sexuality has emerged from the "natural" instinctive need of man to provide a prolongation of himself. Sexuality primarily comes out of the need for physiological reassurance that man's ego will "be saved," even if only in the form of his alter-ego (for example, his descendants), thus remaining in existence in eternity. This would allow us to argue that same-sex marriage is not acceptable (i.e., is not "natural") not only because it is perverted or fails to serve any natural purpose, but because it serves an intrinsic *self-love*, which is related to death. For now, we can affirm that since this relationship is not *"tuned"* to bring about other particularities through reproduction—as is the case with the male-female relation—its main goal is exclusively a *hedonistic* one; φιλαυτία, or self-love, has invented again another clever way to achieve pleasure. "The ego is a wild cat of insatiable appetite," Yannaras concludes.[26]

The problem with the deficient ontology of gender is that relational otherness cannot emerge whenever a *natural quality* is both *archē* and *telos*. The gender relation—although an exciting and promising revelation of otherness[27]—turns out to be a manifestation of utter

---

[24]Ibid., 58. This assertion might be supported by a recent discovery. "One of the great clichés of animal behavior in the context of evolution is that animals act for the good of the species. This idea was discredited in the 1960s but continues to permeate *Wild Kingdom*-like versions of animal behavior. The more accurate view is that animals usually behave in ways that maximize their own reproduction and the reproduction of their close relatives" (Robert Sapolsky, *The Trouble with Testosterone* [New York: Scribner, 1998], 84).

[25]Zizioulas uses the exploration of biologist W. R. Clark. Cf. "On Being Other," n. 134.

[26]Yannaras, *Variations*, 93.

[27]Cf. Yannaras's observations on the ecstatic (from the Greek *ekstasis*, "standing

individualism (and naturalism) and not of an affirmed otherness. *Eros* as sexual attraction is always about feelings and emotions, or goodness, and can be found in the entire animal world, although only in humans embodied in the *self*. (It is interesting that in animals, sexuality is not connected with self, nor is it embodied in the desire of ego.) Gender's "otherness" is always generated or caused by nature and aims at and "rests" in nature. The aesthetic attraction in gender relations serves only as camouflage[28] or decoration, an additional decorative accessory, as a seduction for the final goal: either *reproduction* or the pleasure of self-love. Through evolutionary reflexes of self-preservation and self-survival (of which seduction is one of the components), many species have developed various forms to facilitate this process, so that humankind with such a bodily shape or *eidos* seduces the other gender: "the *desire* for life-in-itself clothes itself in the sex drive."[29] Beauty here is functional for *nature* but not for the person. Otherwise, how does one explain the fact that God loves sinners even more than the righteous ones? It is not a mere accident that the suffering servant from Isaiah 53 "had no form or beauty,"[30] that is, he was aesthetically unacceptable. On the other hand, the resurrected Christ appeared "in another form."[31]

Can we agree, then, that sexual relations—although ecstatic—take place at the level of *nature*, but do not lead to the level of the *mode of being* (personhood)? Whatever the answer is, we see that while the

out") character of *erotic love*, which leads to "personal otherness" (in his *Person and Eros* [Holy Cross Orthodox Press, 2007]), a view that John Zizioulas does not entirely endorse.

[28]"The God of Plato has no freedom, in contrast to the God of Christians who loves sinners and the 'ugly' perhaps even more than those who are 'beautiful and good.'" J. Zizioulas, "'Created' and 'Uncreated,'" in *Communion and Otherness*, 252.

[29]Yannaras, *Relational Ontology*, 24.

[30]Is 53.2.

[31]Mk 16.12.

female "seduces" the man to this "natural" mode of being, the male reduces her to the role of natural child-bearer: in both cases, they are concerned with their own *self*,[32] and for that reason the satisfaction of the drives does not exhaust the *desire*. This is the principal twofold weakness of gender—it aims at and rests in nature, and it cultivates the self at the expense of the Other. On the contrary, Zizioulas asserts, patristic thought proposes "a relational otherness which is always generated or caused by the Other and which aims at and 'rests' in the Other."[33]

Again, the relationship between genders, based on nature, is incapable of producing such a true and, ultimately, particular relationship. Here we must ardently refute the idea that the "natural" way of existence is the authentic form of being,[34] because, as Zizioulas claims, "the only thing that *ultimately* matters in our ethos is the *existence* of the Other."[35] When the natural or moral qualities of the other, whether positive or negative, "good" or "bad," sexual or racial, affect our attitude toward him or her, then we are on an erroneous path of judgmental moralism.

So, if gender is not ontologically justified in its actual condition, let's consider whether or not there is a theology of gender in its eschatological state.

---

[32]This is the conclusion of Denis de Rougemont in *L'Amour et l'Occident* (1939), trans. as *Love in the Western World*.

[33]Zizioulas, "On Being Other," in *Communion and Otherness*, 54.

[34]Cf. Zizioulas's observations in ibid., 64. Zizioulas's *oeuvre théologique* is at its most interesting when attacking such a perception.

[35]Zizioulas, "On Being Other," in *Communion and Otherness*, 91.

Sexuality and Death

We live in a time when relations between the genders (with the "opposite other") have become extremely difficult, not only outside but—we
must acknowledge—even *inside* the Church. This has led to some disturbing practices,[36] and reactions are inevitable. The current ecclesiastical and pastoral reality is often irresolute about gender, about the
"opposite gender," and about women. Yet the Church, as a eucharistic
community, *is* and *must* be the place where otherness of a natural or
social kind, such as the opposition of the sexes, can be transcended.
The transcendence of the biological *hypostasis* and the fear of the
"Other," however, cannot be achieved through man's self-perpetuation in "natural" terms.[37] In the present circumstances (i.e., in our
fallen existence), the relationship between the sexes is "blessed" by the
Church only and exclusively in the form of marriage in the Eucharist.
Actually, sexuality is not a bad thing, but nothing can disengage it from
death. "Nature, the erotic symphony of the prime composer, was and
is a wonderful reverberation of life. A created symphony capable of
echoing the mode of the uncreated, unlimited life. But also capable of

[36]The Orthodox Church is renowned for its traditionalism and faithfulness to
Tradition and has shown this in its position on women's ordination to the priesthood.
Zizioulas holds that this position has resulted, unfortunately, in a commonly held
belief that the Orthodox Church has a rather hostile position to women in general. The
Church canons and traditions are viewed critically because they appear to discriminate against and degrade women. For example, they prohibit women from entering
into the altar, interpret the female monthly cycle as unclean, and so on. These and
similar positions of the Church are used to justify the widespread opinion that women
are rejected in their role and contribution to the life of the Church. These policies,
however, do not represent a strict adherence to "tradition." See his book, Ὀρθοδοξία
καὶ σύγχρονος κόσμος [Orthodoxy and the Modern World] (Nicosia, 2006).

[37]In the humanistic approach, the survival of humankind emerges from faith in
man's inevitable self-perpetuation, whereas in Christian anthropology, it is contingent
and guarantees no survival except insofar as self-perpetuation is in communion with
someone who is not exclusively "natural."

responding musically to the mode of death, the finite self-sufficiency of the created."[38]

Again, sexuality is not bad, but, as modern biology demonstrates, *nothing* can separate it from its impersonal impulses linked to selfish libido. As Yannaras observes,

> The sexual need perpetuates nature, not persons. Our individual existences are of concern to nature only because they channel the genetic material of its own perpetuation: an impersonal supremacy of nature over the personal existences that give it hypostasis. Nature is perpetuated through the endless succession of mortal individuals, and is identified with the survival of the impersonal and undifferentiated; the death of the unique and unrepeatable.[39]

Ontologically Bad but Ethically Good?

For probably the first time in the recent history of theology, theologians (particularly Zizioulas and Yannaras) have begun to treat sex(uality) not as an ethical problem but as an ontological one. This approach changes and affects our general conception of gender and our attitude to sexual relations, and could have immense practical—pastoral and pedagogical—implications for our ecclesial culture. (Today many people go to the monasteries having a vocation for a *parthenikos* [virginal] life but without a clear awareness of the *eschatological* nature of the Church.) One forgets that many prohibitions in the Church—the prohibition of premarital sexual relations, abstinence from sex before the Eucharist, monasticism as a negative position vis-à-vis sex, and so on—are not inspired by ethical motives, but by ontological ones. *Something can be ontologically bad, and ethically good*, and vice versa. However, as

[38]Yannaras, *Variations*, 105.
[39]Ibid., 135.

Zizioulas rightly points out, "in not condemning sexual reproduction as evil and even calling it 'good' (Chrysostom, *De virg.* PG 48, 550), the[se] Fathers did not free it of its *ontological* repercussions owing to its association with death."[40] Yannaras's analysis is also convincing.

> Nature's auto-eroticism is born of death, and beyond nature is the victory of love over death. "The sons of this age marry and are given in marriage; but those who are accounted worthy to attain to that age and to the resurrection from the dead neither marry nor are given in marriage, for they cannot die any more, because they are equal to the angels and are sons of God, being sons of the resurrection" (Luke 20:34–36). The etiological "for" in the third clause of this passage illuminates the connection between sexual relations and death: In "this age" there are no sexual relations because the consequence of death does not exist. So long as death has dominion over nature, nature survives through its sexual power, and that does not mean that the checking or absence of the sexual urge is sufficient for death to be overcome. But when death is overcome, then sexual relations are superfluous.[41]

If Orthodoxy, as Zizioulas insists, has the right vision of *communion* and *otherness* in its faith and in its eucharistic and ecclesial existence, then it has to enlighten us with regard to gender, and—yes—to transmit this vision to the world. The Eucharist is the place where "perfect love casts out fear."[42] Thus, fear of the other can be overcome only by love for all—that is, through acceptance and affirmation by the Other (God) and of the other, something that is indispensable for our own human otherness.[43] This vision is inspired by and with the

[40]Zizioulas, *Communion and Otherness*, 58.

[41]Yannaras, *Variations*, 139.

[42]1 Jn 4.18.

[43]According to St Maximus, "Perfect love does not split up the one nature of men

eschatological perspective—through an anticipation *hic et nunc* of the true state of being that was introduced by Christ's Resurrection and that will come with the Second Coming of Christ. "For in the resurrection they neither marry nor are given in marriage, but are like angels in heaven."[44] "There is no need for this division to last *perpetually*," says St Maximus the Confessor.[45] Together with Sts Maximus and Gregory of Nyssa, we should stress that the basic presupposition of man's true "being" is not to be found in his historical form, but only in his *eschatological* state, which is anticipated in the Holy Eucharist. Seen in Christological perspective, gender is not an absolute category, but rather, it exists in relation to something else—it is contextual. So, although gender-based relations in history are activated through nature, in the *eschaton* they will not be controlled definitively by nature and, equally important, they will be inactive and useless.

Questions and Implications

While our intention here was to see how *otherness* and *communion* relate to *gender*, with all three concepts being understood in the senses accorded to them by John Zizioulas, it is clear that this problem will be one of the most challenging for theology in the future. More study and consideration will be necessary to show whether or not gender identity (and marriage) is a sort of communion where respective differences (uniqueness and personality) are affirmed through a relationship. That

on the basis of their various dispositions but ever looking steadfastly at it, it loves all men equally. . . . In this way also our Lord and God Jesus Christ, manifesting his love for us, suffered for all mankind" (St Maximus the Confessor, *Chapters on Love* 1.71, English translation from *Maximus Confessor: Selected Writings*, trans. George Berthold, Classics of Western Spirituality [Mahwah, NJ: Paulist Press, 1985], 42–43).

[44]Mt 22.30.

[45]*Amb.* 41 (PG 91:1309A).

is, instead of considering gender (and sexuality) as a threat to otherness, we must examine whether or not it *generates* otherness.

Such a study would tackle the subject of gender in different ways. First, one would look at the biblical background and the Gospel perspective of marriage. This should be assessed from the theological perspective, which entails an ecclesial and eucharistic view of the subject. The Orthodox Church has a strong "personalistic" perspective, which was developed in the patristic period. With the help of the Trinitarian theology of the Greek Fathers (particularly the Cappadocians) and their *ontological* perspective, one can gain a clearer theological perspective of the biblical and Gospel perspectives on gender and otherness.[46]

Next, one must consider the whole subject in the light of the ascetical ethos and the mysteries of the Church. The Church cultivates uniqueness through a eucharistic and "erotic" mode of existence. Since Christ is the unique Other in and through whom all other beings are ontologically loved and existentially sustained, as Zizioulas holds, our particular hypostases (persons) are not absorbed into an abstract idea or deity, but rather healed and transfigured in an intimate relationship with God.

Then, there is the need for a discussion of some of the *sociological* aspects of this problem—the feminist perspective (women's rights and feminism) and some contemporary issues (abortion, homosexuality, *in vitro* fertilization, etc.)—in which observations should be made about the male and female in contemporary society. This discussion will also question whether self-conscious gender is socially

[46]Ontology is informally defined as the philosophical or theological study of "being" or existence, and its basic categories and relationships, for the purpose of determining which entities exist and *how* they exist. Theologically speaking, true ontology is one that refers to true being, i.e., God and his Kingdom. In that sense, only that which survives in the Kingdom possesses true ontology.

constructed and whether the conscious gender of every human being is created through social interaction.

Finally, one undertaking this study would be obliged to deal with the *eschatological* perspective in order to see why marital communion, although inextricably tied to otherness and crucially important for understanding this union in an ecclesiological way, does not exist in the Kingdom.[47] It should be discussed whether or not gender identity (male or female) and sexuality have any place in the *eschaton* (which does not imply that in our fallen existence they are not "good").

Overall, in order to illuminate the entire perspective, the following questions need to be resolved: Does otherness, in embracing gender and aiming at transcending and overcoming it—or even eliminating it—achieve this goal? Is there any room for an eschatology (or metaphysics) of gender? Since, in our human circumstances, love and gender (sexuality) are inextricably intertwined, can they acquire an ontological character and justification—that is, are they mutually conditioned *necessarily*? Is it possible for any gender to obtain a unique identity through love and *eros* and to avoid being distinguished and identifiable only by this natural quality or force (but, instead, through sheer relation)? The future but timely reflection of our modern theologians on these questions would no doubt be invaluable to modern Orthodox Christians and, indeed, to all humanity.

[47] Mt 22.30.

True Freedom as the Conquest of the Self

My old, ambitious self...
—Alice, *Still Alice*, directed by Richard Glatzer

I N THE "ASCETIC" PLOT of his movie *Stalker*,[1] Russian filmmaker Andrei Tarkovsky portrays the passage to freedom as the conquest of the self by walking through the doors of transfiguration. In the film's "zone of alienation," where many strange things happen, three men are traveling, while engaging in many arguments, to reach a place called the "Room." This "Room" is said to grant the wishes of anyone who steps inside. Throughout the film, the guide (Stalker) refers to a man who visited the Room, gained a large sum of money, and then hanged himself when he realized that he had become wealthy instead of bringing his brother back from the dead. His suicide was the result of his guilt: he realized that what he believed to be his good desires were false, and that instead he was, deep down, a slave of money. In one of the simplest films ever made (it is more a parable than science fiction), Tarkovsky raises a serious question, especially since the wishes granted by the Room were not necessarily even consciously expressed wishes, but the true, unconscious, darkest desires of those that came in. Some commentators have already suggested that this

---

[1] *Stalker*, directed by Andrei Tarkovsky (Moscow: Mosfilm, 1979), film.

fantastic presupposition could only be brought to us by some sort of holy fool, endeavoring to help his fellow man, and the deep visionary mystery of faith. Tarkovsky himself confesses, "I'm interested in a hero that goes on to the end despite everything. Because only such a person can claim victory."[2]

There is an intricate relationship between true *freedom* and the notion of the *self*, and both concepts are indispensable parts of today's culture. I will endeavor here to examine this relationship, as well as offering a perspective on an understanding of St Paul's notion of liberation from bondage to decay and into freedom.[3]

Modern science attempts to understand human freedom as a genetically determined neurochemical process. This scientific worldview has influenced modern man in his desire to discover a basic hormonal predisposition for taste, fashion, political choices, concerns, preoccupations, and, finally, religiosity. These genes and hormones could, however, also be examined in light of the anthropological experience of the Church, especially in association with its basic idea of *freedom*. I will attempt to say something on this fundamental and fascinating topic.

Modern science, especially medicine, has not provided satisfactory answers to numerous questions about this issue; for example, when are we responsible for our behavior, and when are we under the influence of biological forces beyond our control? Love and falling in love, the intensity of our spiritual life, and the degree of our aggressive impulses are all examined in light of our cerebral system, our brain structure, which supposedly determines all our individual traits. However, it is exactly *here* that one must ask whether human identity is grounded exclusively in a biological hypostasis. If so, *should* it be this way?

[2] Andrei Tarkovsky, *Sculpting in Time: The Great Russian Filmmaker Discusses His Art*, trans. Kitty Hunter-Blair (Austin: University of Texas Press, 1987); also, Andrei Tarkovsky, *Interviews* (Jackson, MS: University Press of Mississippi, 2006), 33.

[3] Cf. Rom 8.21.

The authentic consciousness of the Church teaches that man maintains homeostasis with nature and receives a foretaste of the Truth and supernatural *powers* (the grace of the Holy Spirit) through the eucharistic and ascetic life, which assist him in his struggle for wholeness against illness and sin. This is because we believe that a *genuinely* healthy man is he whose pulse is in harmony with the eucharistic life of the Church.

I would like to examine here, under the light of this new scientific approach, whether *liberation from bondage to decay* can be achieved *through freedom*, as St Paul suggests in Romans 8.21—specifically liberating the self from its bondage to decay. For the time being, I will ask just the crucial question: why and how should true freedom result in conquest of the self? Is "self" a negative notion? If so, this flies in the face of contemporary civilization, which promotes in all things a culture of preoccupation with the pursuit of happiness and well-being for the self.

The Self as Biochemical Otherness, and Freedom as Transcendent Otherness

From the biblical-patristic perspective, our actual biological state constitutes two different and often opposing components: (a) our fallen natural state (anthropologically and cosmologically defined), which, as a result of the inevitable law of entropy, gravitates toward chaos; and (b) a transcendent instinct toward an authentic existence, which does not desire to know death and decay.

The classic biblical-patristic differentiation between the image (εἰκών) and the likeness ("Let us make man in our image, according to our likeness," from Genesis 1.26) is critical to the assumption that, together with his somatic-physical structure by which he is bound to the world in which he lives, man possesses an instinct toward otherworld-liness, linked to the "image of God" within him. Even contemporary philosophical anthropology positively acknowledges the transcendent dimension of man and links it to his freedom. Man received his "icon" (or image, picture) from the moment of his creation; however, he still has to attain his likeness, which is his eschatological designation that, in a certain sense, already now predetermines him. Thus his first struc-ture, the psycho-physical one (all his genetics, biochemistry, neurol-ogy, and physiology), points to the existence of a being that "naturally" reflects the image of God (λόγος τῆς φύσεως) but "supernaturally" (by means that nature does not provide), that is, through his own free will, becomes a being in the likeness of God.

Contemporary Orthodox theologians have observed that, accord-ing to the ecclesial experience, Christian life is understood not merely as a moral and spiritual reality—contrary to the somatic and physi-ological reality—but as an all-encompassing and complex reality, a God-given life in all its dimensions. Man and the entire cosmos are mutually connected in a mysterious way. And "liberation from bond-age to decay" can be achieved only through freedom.

Why is all of this relevant to the problem of true freedom linked with the conquest of the self? On the one hand, the fall is the outcome of this reduction to biology and biochemistry (the original fall of Adam was linked to him following his biological tendencies). On the other hand, the biochemical identity of man does not allow us to reduce his existential otherness to a mere biological hypostasis—which is a basic tendency of the self.

Within the context of modern discussion about the first-created man, it suffices for our topic to accept Adam as the first being in cre-ation that God personally invited to become a god in communion with him and to thus transcend the death and corruption inherent (as a possibility) in the nature of the world. His subsequent rejection of this invitation represents the "fall." The "fall" in Adam (and in all humanity that came after him) is an attempt to attain one's own self-realization, with the individual's self as the point of reference, which is why it leads to death.

Biochemistry is concerned with the basic, irrational aspect of human nature's self-determination; this is as opposed to the rational or *self-governing* (αὐτεξούσιον) aspect, which is not in the realm of biochemistry. In contrast to the Fathers, the main stream of ancient Greek philosophy did not make use of the term "will" (the idea θέλησις never had a terminological status in Greek philosophy). The Fathers understood that only when we take into account the transcendent impulse and instinct of the free person and also comprehend the importance of the *personal* energies (the *tropos*) can we then arrive at a satisfactory philosophical (and theological and medical) interpretation of human complexity. This is precisely because the interaction of the psychosomatic aspect with otherworldliness constitutes the fullness of man's life.

Following in the footsteps of the saints of the Church, how do we overcome the entropy of biochemistry in light of the fact that spirituality is lived through the ascetic and eucharistic experience? Let's take a closer look.

The Ascetic Ethos in the Conquest of the Self

No other aspect of the life of the Church can deal with this question more appropriately than the one the Church has historically demonstrated to do so—the ascetic ethos that is nurtured by monastic spirituality. The ascetic feat of expectantly enduring the Cross and, consequently, experiencing the Resurrection encompasses the whole person and thus defines the ascetic ethos as one based on the brutal struggle for humanity's wholeness and health.

One contemporary ascetic elder, St Porphyrios, summarizes man's neurobiological status and offers the following directives for his transformation:

> Man is a mystery. We carry within us an age-old inheritance—all the good and precious experience of the prophets, the saints, the martyrs, the apostles, and above all our Lord Jesus Christ; but we also carry within us the inheritance of the evil that exists in the world from Adam until the present. All this is within us, instincts and everything, and all demand satisfaction. If we do not satisfy those internal impulses, they will take revenge at some time, unless, that is, we divert them elsewhere, to something higher, to God.[4]

Without a doubt, spirituality, too, generates an *ethos* as a behavioral habit.

If a faulty function of the hormones—that is, their pathology—leads to the appearance of passions (sufferings), theology and medicine concur that *passions* are "incorrectly programmed hormones," which are actually false substitutes for a healthy state of being. They are, moreover, parasites on man's energy and possibilities, with which God endowed man and with which man can strive toward him and participate in the divine life. Christ came in order to save us from the "curse of the law," from the law that governs the "selfish genes," and from the power of sin, death, and the devil[5]—to grant us true life.

In the light of this insight, the Fathers go on to explain how the cortex exerts restraint on attachments, or on a programmed "misper-

---

[4]St Porphyrios, *Wounded by Love: The Life and Wisdom of Saint Porphyrios*, trans. John Raffan (Limni-Evia: Denise Harvey, 2009), 134.

[5]Cf. Gal 3.13; Heb 2.14–18.

ception," that is, on a passion. They even offer a genealogy of passions. In this vein, St Maximus the Confessor says, "For man's intellect is a holy place and a temple of God in which the demons, having desolated the soul by means of impassioned thoughts, set up the idol of sin."[6] St Maximus' astounding diagnosis is not without a corresponding therapy. To begin with, the Confessor says, "He who drives out self-love, the mother of the passions, will, with God's help, easily rid himself of the rest, such as anger, irritation, rancor, and so on. But he who is dominated by self-love is overpowered by the other passions, even against his will."[7] As long as self-love exists, the other passions have an entrée.

How can a passionate thought become a dispassionate thought and, therefore, free from passion—that is, separated from a wrong perception? An impassioned conceptual image is "a thought compounded of passion and a conceptual image. If we separate the passion from the conceptual image, what remains is the passion-free thought. We can make this separation by means of spiritual love and self-control, if only we have the will."[8]

It follows from this analysis that the natural impulse of man cannot produce a passion if man's "ego" does not *desire* it. Consequently, self-love is the root and cause of all problems and also of the capricious passions, because in the fallen state they appear as a separate self (in psychological terms, a detached self) that is concerned only with "itself." As such, it pertains to the *soul* and subjects everyone and everything to its *own* judgment, nurturing the deceitful idea of its own idealized image. This causes a strange law in human behavior. "For I delight in the law of God, in my inmost self, but I see in my members

---

[6] St Maximus, *On Love* 2.31.
[7] Ibid. 2.8.
[8] Ibid. 3.43.

another law (ἕτερον νόμον) at war with the law of my mind and making me captive to the law of sin which dwells in my members."[9]

If we were to apply these truly elementary insights to the neurobiology of man who has entered into communion with the Church, a very interesting picture would emerge.

The Conquest of the Selfish Genes in the Community of the Church

In order to discover the roots underlying this somatic and spiritual convergence, we first need to understand that in patristic writings about the somatic aspect, the negative statements about the body are not a negation of the body *as such*. Instead, it is because the somatic aspect can make a "fortress of individualism" and an armor for the self that it can be problematic.

This problem is of such significance that it cannot be circumvented; however, the answer is found in Christology.

Compared to us, Christ's hypostasis is not a hypostasis derived from a biological existence, but rather from a free and divine existence, and therefore it is possible for him to have a body and to be the Savior of the world. In Christ we see what a transcended biological existence is. His "mode of existence" is such that it modifies the requirements of the "law of nature" without abolishing the body and its instincts, but redirects the same toward the truly Desired One. Whoever is grafted onto that hypostasis (is "hypostasized into") inside his Body, through baptism and Eucharist, has the opportunity to "immerse" his biochemical and psychological individuality in a new life of freedom and grace. Since in Christ there is in an indivisible union with the Holy Spirit, which, according to Paul's ecclesiology, signifies the *community*,

[9]Rom 7.22–23.

this communion results in the "communion of the saints" who, though experiencing the tragedy of existence within the framework of history, overcome it through the foretaste of Truth encountered in the Holy Eucharist.

Here we come to see the crucial importance of the Church. Why does the Church matter? In the communion of the Church, the Holy Eucharist offers the only occasion in history where individualism and the self are healed in such a radical way. In the Eucharist, the "Body of Christ," both individually and ecclesiologically, is the *gathering* that is irreducible to its basic elements. Hence, soteriological assumptions in anthropology cannot be made outside the Holy Eucharist. This represents a revolution in the history of thought, because the human subject is not regarded as a separate subject (a detached self) but as an "I" who loves and is loved by the community of "the first-born among many brethren."[10] The grace-filled consequences for man's true life of "being in communion" are assured. Love and freedom, the two key components of an authentic therapy, can overcome one's own pathology only in a deeply involved relationship, where love overcomes biological selectiveness and narcissism, and freedom becomes freedom for the other. As a result, the Holy Eucharist, which is for healing and for life eternal, eliminates our desire for death by not allowing the fusion of being and nonbeing, life and death, which is characteristic of our biochemical existence.

What kind of experience regarding the true person does the ecclesial hypostasis give us? By becoming a member of a community of relations, the Church (which supersedes the exclusiveness of nature, class, race, gender, and other aspects), man *learns to love and to extend his love beyond nature* (and even beyond aesthetics, *eros*, and class); that is, he is free from the law of his biological nature (individualism).

[10]Rom 8.29.

The only aspect of his biological nature from which he cannot yet be freed is death. As long as death has not been finally overcome, the ailing biochemistry will continue to last. That's why St Paul says that the entire creation awaits liberation from bondage to decay, through the freedom of the children of God.[11]

In modern terms, the recognition that the greater part of human consciousness is a natural-biological product does not cancel out the truth that God is able to "touch" the existential chords of man that are beyond neurobiological processes. "The Divine itself is subject to movement since it produces an inward state of intense longing (erotic force) and love in those receptive to them; it moves others, since by nature it attracts the desire of those who are drawn toward it."[12] Thus grace, as the personal visitation of God, awakens one's freedom, which, now renewed and sanctified (and filled), opposes the "will of the flesh"—those absolute natural desires resistant to spiritual life—that had overpowered the free will by conquering one's internal space.

Conclusions

These theological insights, translated into the language of ecclesiastical therapeutics, demonstrate that the wholeness of man depends on several fundamental conditions. Here are the basic conclusions to be drawn from this important subject:

1. The only authentic way out of the vicious circle of our biochemical predicament is by connecting it with Christology and ecclesiology—that is, with the life of the Holy Mysteries of the Church. It is possible to arrive at this mode (*tropos*) only because the human person has a reference, a reference *pointing* to a factor outside the human

[11]Cf. Rom 8.21.
[12]St Maximus (PG 91:1260C).

being and hence to an uncreated ontology, which is the existence of God.

2. This mode cannot be realized within the framework of history without suffering (πάθος). Specifically, since the human psychophysical structure is in a "fallen" state, man inevitably has to go the way of the Cross, through the *narrow gates* that lead into the Kingdom. Freedom from "selfish genes" and "narcissistic" molecules, achieved by the saints, is only possible by not avoiding a *martyrdom* and by the honest acceptance of human limitations and weaknesses. By experiencing their own infirmities through the foretaste of the gift of the Kingdom, the ascetics experienced such love that it could be celebrated as the greatest of all.[13]

3. The Church has offered both baptism and the Eucharist as two Mysteries through which we can overcome our fallen biochemistry. In baptism, the person is immersed into Christ's death, that is, the actual death of the old man and of his "methods of knowledge" and natural passions. Resurrecting as a new man with Christ, continually renewed and transfigured in the image of Christ, the God-Man, and, according to the Apostle Paul, acquiring a *new mind*, the *"mind of Christ,"*[14] the person emerges from the baptismal font free to participate fully in the life of Christ through receiving the Holy Eucharist.

4. The Eucharist does not only give a foretaste, but perhaps even more importantly provides a *surety* for eschatological health and healing. The Eucharist, administered correctly, is a place of healing, not because it offers immediate "alleviation" but because it is a "medicine of immortality" that has a long-term effect—as a surety of future health—and which is received as a gift by the community and the persons therein. By virtue of being the *place* of healing, it is the *manner*

[13]Cf. 1 Cor 13.8–13.
[14]1 Cor 2.16.

by which one moves from self-love to the love of God and to brotherly love.

5. One can acknowledge the existence of a biochemistry of the *gnomic* will or *proairesis*,[15] but not a biochemistry of *freedom* (or even natural will), since the latter evades biochemistry in a manner that is both mysterious and experientially real, mainly because of God's salvific action and his transforming presence in us and among us. [16]

There is no such thing as a hopeless determinism that reduces freedom to impulses and instincts. Although God in Christ constantly sends us his loving, transcendent invitation, he does not forcefully impose happiness on us; instead "the Spirit himself intercedes for us with sighs too deep for words,"[17] and only Christ with the Holy Spirit has the key to the riddle of the mystery of salvation, healing, and the purpose of man's existence in history.

[15]"Therefore, will (θέλησις) is not *proairesis*, if will (θέλησις) is a simple rational and vital desire, whereas *proairesis* is a combination of desire, deliberation, and judgment. For it is after first desiring that we deliberate, and after deliberating that we judge, and after judging that we deliberately choose what has been shown by judgment better rather than worse. And will (θέλησις) is related only to what is natural, whereas *proairesis* is related to [or depends on] what is up to us and capable of being brought about through us." St Maximus the Confessor, *Opusc.* 1 (PG 91:12C–13A).

[16]This is developed more extensively in my studies, "Is There a Biochemistry of Freedom?", *History, Truth, Holiness: Studies in Theological Ontology and Epistemology* (Alhambra, CA: Sebastian Press, 2011), 67–117; and "Truth and History: Implications in Theology and Science," *History, Truth, Holiness,* 21–51.

[17]Rom 8.26.

PART III

Mercy, Law, and Council

"All of Us Are Beggars"

THEOLOGICAL FOUNDATIONS
OF PHILANTHROPY

I n *The Soloist*, a 2009 British-American drama film directed by Joe
Wright, a moving relationship is described between a homeless
musician and a *Los Angeles Times* columnist. Nathaniel Ayers, played
by Jamie Foxx, is a musician who has become homeless after develop-
ing schizophrenia, and Steve Lopez, played by Robert Downey Jr., is
trying to help him. At one point, Steve's doctor encourages Steve to
continue to be a friend to Ayers and says: "Relationship is primary. . . .
It is possible to cause seemingly biochemical changes through human
emotional involvement. You literally have changed his chemistry by
being his friend."[1]

Along similar lines, in this essay we address the Christian mandate
to engage the world with the charity of God within the framework of an
Orthodox theological dialogue. In the contemporary secular context,
which eschews theology in favor of service, philanthropy is divorced
from ecclesiology. Yet, the Church does not minister to humanity
because externals inspire it to do so, but because it is the life of the
Holy Trinity manifest through service. Humanitarianism that is a *consequence* of the Trinitarian and incarnational aspect of the Church's
body and of its relational nature in the Spirit is prepared to serve as

---

[1] *The Soloist*, directed by Joe Wright (Hollywood, CA: Paramount Home Entertainment, 2009), film.

the hands of God during a crisis. Humanitarianism that is market-driven is subject to the amoral logic that drives the market. The true Christian finds life in charity. Through charity, he or she encounters the animating power of the Holy Trinity, similar to what happened on a psychological level to Nathaniel in *The Soloist*.

Incarnate theology cultivates social and political action creatively. The undeniable crisis of the modern cultural paradigm is how to invite churches to break out of their comfort zone and engage. Broadly speaking, ecclesial philanthropy must be situated within the context of both Trinitarian and Christological theology; absent this context, every social dynamic is subordinated to an exclusive economy that represents itself as the only criterion for social "development." In moving beyond utilitarianism,[2] Christian philanthropy articulates its *differentia specifica*. Without such an articulation, Christian philanthropy will wither.

In the minds of some people, the Orthodox are involved in social movements merely to project "contemporariness" by mimicking foreign social patterns. Even those with the best intentions and real respect for Orthodoxy would find it difficult to answer the question, "What is the real contribution the Orthodox Church can make to humanitarianism?" Orthodox Christians appear to be appeased by a lovely liturgy and seem steadfastly unwilling to draw societal and ethical implications from it. This kind of mindset suggests a dialectical thinking that ignores or denies the complementarity of worship and service. Instead, let us look for and gather what is unique about Orthodox humanitarianism.

Humanitarianism is neither a postmodern invention nor a strictly Western phenomenon. The extensive range of social-theological theories and documents produced by the Roman Catholic Church in

---

[2]"Utilitarian," e.g., the necessity for organizing social life, achievement of a certain purpose, etc.

the last two centuries should not blind us to or intimidate us from also observing the rich nexus of philanthropic welfare systems in the Eastern Roman (Byzantine) Empire, which in retrospect was called "Byzantium." While Orthodoxy does not have a developed and marketed "social theory" or comprehensive "social dossier," the Orthodox Church certainly has a worldview about such vital problems, especially since these social crises are central to the Gospel *kērygma*, or teaching. There are also Orthodox patristic texts on social welfare that counter both modern practical solutions and early medieval Byzantine philanthropy by offering the self-evident explanation for *why mercy ought to be shown to others*. Modern scholarship on the subject[3] has also demonstrated that the explanation for *why mercy ought to be shown to others* was self-evident within the social context of Byzantium that was formed by Christian values, although "it was not at all self-evident to classical society."[4]

In an age where many kinds of people exercise their responsibility to help the needy, there are no reasons, theological or otherwise, preventing the Orthodox from robust participation in public life. Still, participation in public life and service requires understanding why one is acting. Presently, in the Orthodox Church, philanthropy, in its social dimension, has become divorced from ecclesiology. The Orthodox somehow feel socially *obligated* to put forth their philanthropy as a model and example for society. This is wrong. The Church should

[3] See, for example, Bishop Danilo Krstić, *On Divine Philanthropy: From Plato to John Chrysostom* (Los Angeles: Sebastian Press, 2012); and Matthew J. Pereira, ed., *Philanthropy and Social Compassion in Eastern Orthodox Tradition: Papers of the Sophia Institute Academic Conference, New York, Dec. 2009* (New York: Theotokos Press, 2010).

[4] McGuckin, "Embodying the New Society: The Byzantine Christian Instinct of Philanthropy," in *Philanthropy and Social Compassion*, 51 (also in *Illumined in the Spirit: Studies in Orthodox Spirituality*, vol. 3 of *The Collected Studies of John A. McGuckin* [Yonkers, NY: St Vladimir's Seminary Press, 2017], 199–218, at 200).

not act in this or that way because externals inspire it, but because it is an image and a sign of the Holy Trinity. Only if humanitarianism is a *consequence* of the Trinitarian and incarnational aspect of the Church's body and of its relational nature in the Spirit can Orthodox Christians then serve as hands of God during a crisis.

The divorce of philanthropy and ecclesiology has arisen because worship and social action are seen as two opposite spheres. In the liturgical perspective—and Liturgy is a social event *par excellence*—the Church and the world are not ontologically separated. However, while seeing history as the arena for man's struggle with social evil, we should not overlook the fact that the Church's main task is ultimately the *struggle with corruption and death*. Conversely, the Church's focus on the Kingdom should not undermine its incarnational mission to be involved in history.

Part of the philanthropic dimension of this mission is a profound care for creation. This stewardship is not simply a *desideratum* of social polity,[5] but a consequence of the transformation of humanism by theo-humanism, such as that described by St Justin of Ćelije.[6] The Orthodox Church does not act merely according to Western, goal-oriented criteria and utilitarian approaches. Yet, this is difficult for Western critics to take into account; this is in part because the West today risks confusing ecclesiology with sociology, "because it has lived for so long without the East reminding it of the utter *dialectic* between God and the world."[7] The free exchange between the Divine and the created in the

[5]See McGuckin, preface to *Philanthropy and Social Compassion*, 9.

[6]"In all cultures and civilizations, all the torments of the human spirit ultimately merge into one gigantic effort: to overcome death and mortality, and to ensure immortality and life, to ensure it at any price." Justin Popovich, *Man and the God-Man* (Los Angeles: Sebastian Press, 2009), 18.

[7]John D. Zizioulas, *The One and the Many: Studies on God, Man, the Church, and the World Today* (Los Angeles: Sebastian Press, 2010), 135.

Person of Christ necessitates an evaluation of the exchange between Orthodox theory and praxis.

In an era in which human persons are exposed to destructive or hurtful practices, the unique responsibility of protecting the sanctity of the person is even more urgent. Philanthropy is both a deep theological task and a persistent social demand, and theology and praxis must be united in *philanthrōpia*.

Divine Philanthropy: Holy Trinity

Human philanthropy cannot be detached from divine philanthropy. This is a simple yet critical realization, one that implies that ecclesial philanthropy must occur within Trinitarian theology. The genuinely human task of responding to horizontal social issues is inspired and informed by the verticality of the Trinitarian faith. Yet, the dignity of personhood is grounded not in an abstract divinity but in the life of the three Persons.

The Persons of the Holy Trinity provide the basis for Orthodox humanitarianism foremost through the recognition that Christian philanthropy and anthropology are linked with Christology, because Christology is inseparable from Triadology. Such a link is not merely *monistic*: as "one of the Trinity," Christ, "the anointed one," is from the Father and in the Holy Spirit.[8] God's revelation of the fullness of his Being as the Holy Trinity, this Tri-Personal revelation of God—through the doctrine of the *imago Dei*—is relevant to society: "God who is personal and . . . is not a person confined in his own self" is

---

[8]"The name of Christ represents the complete confession of our Faith because it shows God (the Father) Who anointed Him, and the Son Who was anointed and the Holy Spirit Who is the Ointment [χρῖσμα, Chrism], as we have learned from the Apostle Paul in Acts: 'How God anointed Jesus Christ from Nazareth with the Holy Spirit' (Acts 10.38)" (St Basil the Great [PG 32:116]).

a mysterious "model" for the plurality of coequal and unique human persons, as well as for their consubstantial Adamic unity of nature."[9]

This unity of human nature does not reduce distinction, however; rather, the Trinitarian doctrine reveals that communion in the Holy Trinity does not threaten otherness, but *generates* it. Zizioulas contributes to this consideration of the uniqueness of personhood in the Holy Trinity when he observes that uniqueness is not achieved by way of variance in properties, but by way of the simple affirmation of being who he is within the context of relationship. Father, Son, and Holy Spirit are all names indicating relationship and otherness. No person can be "other" unless he or she is related to another.[10]

As a body of relationships, the Church is organized and functions in the world as an expression of the life of the Holy Trinity. This is not a *social trinitarianism* but, instead, an affirmation of love that is grounded in the self-emptying of Christ's kenotic example. The Orthodox Church does not reduce its understanding of the Trinity to social models and sociological paradigms. It does not aim to borrow from sociology when discussing and implementing divine philanthropy. In this regard, sociological models can only be enriched by drawing from theology.[11] The Trinitarian doctrine teaches us to live as persons rather than as individuals, since persons are creatures of relationship and not isolated and "independent" beings. Persons can live in the midst of torture and the threat of self-extinction because they exist within the relational, love-based life of the Church. Individuals do not. This is why individuals will wilt in the midst of persecution by the state, but the Church can still operate under such conditions, or even when no state

[9]Krstić, *On Divine Philanthropy*, 46.
[10]This is a classic Zizioulas argumentation in his *Communion and Otherness*.
[11]We exclude any possibility of explaining the Trinity on the basis of human societal nature.

exists.[12] This leads to the revelation of personal uniqueness, otherness, and freedom even through social relations. The rich fabric of human dignity is social, since the "sociality" of the Holy Trinity is God's mark on all creation. The logic inherent in such an attitude elicited a basic imperative in the ancient Church, both in practice and theory: being a person means to exist in *communion*. But it also means to exist in a *sacrificial* way.

Integral to the sacrificial quality of existence is salvation; since divine *philanthrōpia* specifies the detailed method by which *oikonomia* works, it provides an ecclesiological framework for understanding how deeply God is transmitting his influence on any particular person or act. Only the Life-creating Trinity can restore the original foundation of the person and thereby redeem existence. It is only through such a redemption that one develops a more refined concern for society. Thus, *philanthrōpia* cannot be an abstract label for virtue, because the Orthodox social commitment and engagement is exemplified only within the Holy Trinity.

To one extent or another, this view of philanthropy is one held by many, if only implicitly. However, the Holy Trinity's exemplification of social commitment leads to emphatically distinguishing the *person-centered* mentality from the *individual-centered* mentality. Our

[12]Vladan Perišić (*Theological Disambiguations*, 259) has provided an exceptional example of the connection between personal otherness and martyrdom: "It is *possible* to realize one's true self (I am not saying it is *necessary* or *desirable*) even in those situations in which there are no 'human rights.' I shall give just one example: martyrs were martyrs precisely because they had no human rights—often not even the right to live. (We can also put it like this: the deprivation of their human rights gave them the opportunity to be martyrs.) A world without human rights is really a terrible one, but even in such a world one can be a true human. Moreover, *prima facie* paradoxically, a world deprived of human rights has often been a chance for every human in their everyday life with other people—to prove that they really are *humans*." The Church's Christ-likeness exists above politics in the fulfillment of true humanism.

argument for the dignity of the human person exceeds the *individual-centered* approach in order to discover its ultimate unquantifiable value in the three Persons.[13]

The Holy Trinity expressively contours the model for an élan of compassion among men, inspiring praxis and shaping our broader Orthodox social vision. In that sense, everything that *depersonalizes* the human being—poverty, violence, and, above all, death—manifests the indifference of humanity. Lethargy and apathy about such social issues then emerge as passions hostile to the cradle of creation. Care for men should not be transformed into impersonal social institutions and structures intended only for economic and cultural development. Such development dehumanizes and can justify perverse means to an improperly conceived end.

The archetype of philanthropic exercise in early Christianity was an icon of the Trinity or an icon of Christ's kenosis. In *kenotic* and *eschatological* ecclesiology, one observes that *kenōsis* never reduces philanthropy to mere charitable patronage. Rather, the salvific power of Christ is communicated in the exchange. One should ultimately become a brother or sister to the one wounded by the side of the road, whom we help because the person has been brought into the Church, which is the House of Healing. In the Church, all are brothers and sisters who share the same Father. The parable of the Good Samaritan, in this respect, provides the model for Christian philanthropy. The pedagogical function is to encourage us to act like the Good Samaritan: "You go, and do likewise."[14] Additionally, the patristic understanding sees Christ as the Good Samaritan and each Christian as the wounded

[13]Personhood in this approach does not lead back to substances (as in Aristotle) or ideals (as in Plato) but other persons in harmonious, loving existence of difference and interdependence.

[14]Lk 10.37.

traveler. Christ cleans, anoints, and binds our wounds and takes us to the inn of the Church for safekeeping before promising to the innkeeper, his bishop, the administrator of the Church: "I will repay you when I come back." This promised return refers to Christ's return at the eschaton. The *eschaton* serves as propellant to philanthropic exercise. Self-emptying and the Second Cóming are, therefore, harmoniously combined.

Incarnational (Christological) Philanthropy

The Trinity-inspired compassion of man toward man is then the ideal by which we must evaluate humanitarianism. But before examining the connection between human persons and the personal existence of the Holy Trinity as revealed in the Son, let us clarify the notion of the Son's *oikonomia*.

The Greek word *oikonomia* originates from St Paul (see Eph 3.2–9; Col 1.25, "the administration of God's grace" or "the stewardship of the mystery") and is widely used by the Holy Fathers, especially in ecclesiological-canonical texts.[15] The divine-human economy is the foundation of Christianity, the basis and being of the Church itself. The Church is created and exists through the *oikonomia* of the Incarnation, Passion, and Resurrection of Christ, for us men and for our salvation. St Basil the Great wrote about this in his *Letter to Christians in Tyana*, reminding them that we "stand more in need of the succor of each of the brethren than one hand does of the other."[16] Such succor, one would say, stands as the support and means through which God's grace is communicated.

[15]Bishop Atanasije Jevtić, *Contemporary Ecclesiological Reminder on the Diaspora* [in Serbian] (Los Angeles: Sebastian Press, 2014), 67.

[16]Basil, *Letter 97*. And he asserts, "The Lord Himself undertook the *economy*, that by the blood of His cross He might make peace between things in earth and things in heaven."

This reasoning is sound, as far as it goes, but it misses the real intent of the "Cappadocian" notion of *oikonomia*. The Cappadocians (Sts Basil the Great, Gregory the Theologian) and St John Chrysostom emphasize that only a correct understanding of the *oikonomia* (or economies) of God illuminates the genuine nature of love for one's neighbor. Love for one's neighbor motivates the sympathetic response in every aspect of human weakness. St Gregory's eulogization of *philoptochia* ("love of the poor," in his *Oration 14*) eloquently testifies to sympathy. Knowing that "all of us are beggars and needy of divine grace [the Holy Spirit]"[17] makes it easier to express empathy and, at some level, identify ourselves with "the utter misery of the destitute." In *Oration 14*, St Gregory the Theologian elaborated on the idea by suggesting that human empathy makes one most resemble God. With this insight, St Gregory was able to invoke a Christological anthropology to profound effect that has, as we will see, *social verification*.[18] So he insists, "Let us take care of Christ while there is still time, let us feed Christ, let us clothe Christ, let us gather Christ in, let us show Christ honor . . . through the needy, who are today cast down on the ground."[19] The "us" that St Gregory addresses is, indeed, the Church of Christ.

Beyond giving society a theologically graceful, conceptually authoritative, and, for the first time, fully consistent theory of philanthropy, the Cappadocian concept of an *ecclesial economy* also thoroughly reshaped our view of social *differences*. It is the Church that receives *everyone*, especially sinners, and that looks up to Christ—the "meek and humble in heart," as the good Samaritan who "pours out oil

[17] *Or*. 14.1.

[18] "By the fifth [century], bishops had entered philanthropic work so fundamentally into the ecclesial substructure that they had earned the common-parlance title of *Philoptochos* (friend of the poor)." (McGuckin, "Embodying the New Society," in *Philanthropy and Social Compassion*, 52.

[19] *Or*. 14.40.

and wine" on human wounds. Therefore, a Christological *philanthrōpia* conveys societal concern through gifts of charity, liberation of the slaves, public help, or the expression of a quality opposed to miserliness. Furthermore, by becoming a member of an ecclesial community of relations—which supersedes the exclusiveness of natural, social, racial, gender, and other aspects—man learns to love and to extend his love *beyond nature* (aesthetics, *eros*, class, status); that is, he is free from the law of his biological nature—his old ambitious self, marked by individualism.

Clearly, this is a radically different way of thinking about humanitarianism. But it is anchored in the simple recognition that, within the Church, man acquires the habit of loving and learns how to be loved only when it is done freely and without exclusion. This is a community in which, according to St Maximus the Confessor, "perfect love does not divide the nature of man . . . but always embracing it, loves all men equally. . . . For our God and Lord Jesus Christ showed his Love to us by suffering for all of humanity. . . ."[20] By suffering for all humanity, Christ's Passion implies that there cannot be love that is not *socially oriented*. This proportional relationship between philanthropy and salvation leads directly to ecclesiology.

Ecclesial and Eucharistic Philanthropy

A point that is overlooked and hardly ever taught by our contemporaries is that "philanthropy in Orthodox culture is not merely an ethical or societal phenomenon: rather it is part of the great *Mysterion* of Christ's presence in the world."[21] As part of Christ's earthly ministry, philanthropy is intrinsic to all who would be Christ-like.

---

[20]St Maximus, *On Love* 1.71. Also see *Epist. 2* (*On Love*).

[21]Matthew Pereira, editor's preface, in *Philanthropy and Social Compassion*, 14.

Therefore, it is hasty and historically unjustified to conclude that the concept of social compassion is absent from Eastern theology. This does not mean that the participation in "social struggles" (as they are known in our age since we have come upon our own panoply of social issues) was a defining attribute of Byzantium, since, normally, cognizance of evil in social structures was not established in that period. On the other hand, the Byzantine ascetic tradition made it clear that passage (*pascha*) to the Kingdom involved going through the *sacrifice* in the history of salvation.[22] Social compassion in ecclesial life combines the stability of Christological truth and the spontaneity of the grace of the Holy Spirit. Thus, *ecclesial* social activism does not result from social experience but from a sacramental taste of the life of God. Philanthropy cannot, therefore, be detached from the eucharistic mystery.

This conclusion should be a cause for celebration among supporters of a more broadly defined *activist* outlook. Since eucharistic worthiness is "bound up with neighborly love,"[23] we are forced to expand the notion of Liturgy to "before" and "after": not only "Liturgy *after* the Liturgy," but also Liturgy *before* the Liturgy. St John Chrysostom calls the poor the "living altar of the body of Christ."[24] As the bearer of the sacrifice, the altar is the cradle of he through whom death was, is, and shall be overthrown.

It is exactly this background against which the ecclesial leaders in Byzantium and medieval Serbia developed a complex program of philanthropic activities in many urban centers. While I was a monk in Herzegovina, Bishop Atanasije taught us that the monastery in which

---

[22]Cf. John D. Zizioulas, *The One and the Many: Studies on God, Man, the Church, and the World Today* (Los Angeles: Sebastian Press, 2010), 36.

[23]Ibid., 8.

[24]*Homilies on Matthew* 50.3–4 (PG 58:508).

we lived (Tvrdoš Monastery, Herzegovina) belonged to the tradition of the famous Nemanjić dynasty, which emphasized hospitality and always prioritized the reception of guests even over individual prayer. Should we conclude, then, that prayer is less important? Rather than being parts of a hierarchy of priority, hospitality complements prayer. Hospitality can even be an expression of prayer.

There is something else of importance that all theologians, regardless of their provenance, also agree upon. It is implicit in what we have described, but it is worth stating directly. The experience of divine philanthropy is acquired, according to the Church Fathers, by "dying" for others and by loving one's *enemies,* and thereby not permitting the "fragmentation of human nature." It is striking how in Jesus' parable of the rich man and Lazarus the word "chasm"[25] is explicitly applied to describe an existential situation and is not only applied to the chasm existing between the wealthy and the poor. The rich man in the Gospel parable lived his whole life with a great *ontological* chasm between him and poor Lazarus. Lazarus was next to him, but an unbridgeable chasm separated them. By not accommodating the poor in his communion, the rich man acted in an *anti-eucharistic* way.

The constructive interconnection between the Eucharist and *agapē* generates a social dynamic able to transfigure social incentives into an Orthodox praxis. The consequences of a eucharistic social consciousness of the Church are thus far-reaching and should be constantly emphasized.

Eschatological Philanthropy

Given that ecclesial philanthropy is, as we have seen, a matter of *personal* love and not of natural compassion, we have to find its escha-

---

[25]χάσμα μέγα, Lk 16.26.

tological rationale. We are not dealing with a genuinely outreaching altruistic philosophy, but with a *relational eschatological ontology*, because "only that which survives at the end possesses true being."[26] Only in that way can *philanthropy* be "seen as a highly charged Eschatological reality."[27] What we are talking about is actually an eschatologically inspired compassion.

This eschatological outlook requires a dramatic change in our thinking. Because true compassion is eschatologically inspired, sociology cannot supplant ecclesiology. The dialectic between history and the *eschaton* prohibits a lifeless escape from the tribulations of the "here and now." The eschatological is always *relational*, and the relational forms a sociology informed by the Divine *oikonomia*. But to see Truth from an *activistic* perspective is to misunderstand it. It must be viewed, rather, "as *the taste of an existence* in which whatever is achieved in history is shown to be transcended eschatologically."[28] This simple idea actually allows us to capture the core insight of ecclesial humanitarianism: as long as the goal and axis of collectiveness is eschatological and not utilitarian, social activism is eschatologically justified.

Implications for Ecclesial Philanthropy Today

The classic Byzantine approach to the theology of compassion—the sentiment that one is saved through benevolent action toward the desperately needy—has only recently taken root in the modern Orthodox "social consciousness" of today. This early Christian and Byzantine "instinct of philanthropy" *should* be transmitted and adopted by contemporary Christians. We must recognize, though, how the cultural and societal framework shapes the way people help each other

---

[26]Zizioulas, *Communion and Otherness*, 60.

[27]Pereira, editor's preface, in *Philanthropy and Social Compassion*, 9.

[28]Zizioulas, *The One and the Many*, 60.

today, as Christians in ancient Greco-Roman society did. The ecclesial parish (or diocese) is an ideal possibility for where the fulfillment of personal-philanthropic authenticity could take place, centered on the image of the "Christ-poor as altar."[29]

There is a deeper and more profound understanding of person-hood that is revealed when we take into account the intermingling of the divine Person with a human. The Trinitarian and Christological image of philanthropy affirms that the Persons of the Holy Trinity are the model for the understanding of man. In what way is it possible for the Persons of the Holy Trinity to form such a basis? When any humanitarian or sociological concept of person is examined in the light of the Holy Trinity, then the concept of "philanthropy" is eluci-dated existentially and sociologically. And through this, the mystical dignity of the person is affirmed.

The affirmation of personhood does not endanger philanthropy nor the Church, which is its true cradle; the real risk occurs when one thinks that philanthropic work *exhausts* one's existence or essence. According to St Gregory the Theologian, "you will not pose any dan-ger to yourself by doing this. . . . [C]ome to his help, offer him nour-ishment, offer her a scrap of clothing, provide medicine, bind up his wounds, ask something about her condition, offer sage advice about endurance, give encouragement, be a support."[30]

Thornier issues arise, though, when we think about the place of philanthropy in modern technology. A careful examination of the patristic use of the term *philanthrōpia* (especially in St Gregory's *Ora-tion 14*) shows that it was associated with the poor and the sick, but—this is important—it included "those who were suffering all types of evils, whether long or short term, in a way which suppressed one's

[29]St John Chrysostom, *Homilies on Matthew* 50.3–4 (PG 58:508).
[30]*Or.* 14.27.

dignity."[31] In society today, technology is often employed to deperson-alize and suppress dignity. In his book, *The Death of the Neighbor*,[32] Luigi Zoja discusses how modern technology has eradicated the sec-ond Judeo-Christian commandment: *Love thy neighbor as thyself.* In this technological, mass civilization, we do not care about our neigh-bors, and most often we do not even know if our neighbor is dying. On the other hand, technology helps us act quickly to help "neighbors" who might be physically far away. For example, GoFundMe recently facilitated the rapid collection of much-needed money for the family of a newly departed Orthodox priest by reaching out to a network of persons through social media websites.

It is not enough for Christians to unite in the struggle for social issues, however. We look at salvation not only as a response to social welfare—transcending social injustice, hunger, oppression, and other social ills—but as a matter of ontology, as transcendence of corruption and death. Consequently, the Church "that serve[s] social utility and the rational regulation of rights and desires, or the relations between work and capital, has nothing to do with theology."[33]

The transformative ontology of Orthodox humanitarianism also has ecological implications because the "chasm" between the rich man and Lazarus is of cosmic significance. Beyond the ideological commit-ment to global environmental wholeness, the Orthodox are mindful of the eucharistic and ascetical approach to the natural environment. Our compassion cannot fail to be expanded to include all of God's innocent

---

[31]Vicki Petrakis, "*Philanthropia* as a Social Reality of *Askesis* and *Theosis* in Greg-ory the Theologian's Oration: *On the Love of the Poor*," in *Philanthropy and Social Compassion*, 99.

[32]Luigi Zoja, *La morte del prossimo* (Torino: Einaud, 2009).

[33]Christos Yannaras, *The Meaning of Reality: Essays on Existence and Commu-nion, Eros and History* (Los Angeles: Sebastian Press, 2011), 150.

creation. Humanitarianism must include caring for the environment in which we live and upon which we depend for our survival.

Some Christian charitable endeavors have sown confusion and led to misunderstandings. On the one hand, the Church should do its charitable social acts (or any ethical or political act) *with a caveat.* Namely, if we endanger the basic, ultimate concerns by simply mimicking other social programs, then we are engaged in a sociology detached from ecclesiology. On the other hand, caring solely about eschatology while giving the cold shoulder to those in need is also not the position of the Church. Can a cold shoulder reach across the chasm? Those in the Church who fight for social justice must appreciate the existential importance of social struggles so that the Church will maintain a *prophetic* disposition, forever keeping in mind a time of judgment for all actions.

Sharing the eucharistic bread reveals the energetic renewal of social compassion's joy as it spreads from face to face like candlelight spreading from taper to taper in Pascha's predawn. The proper basis for joyful humanitarianism is the same as the basis for our understanding of God: personhood.

Idealizing Politics Abolishes the Eschaton

ON DEMOCRACY, HUMAN RIGHTS, AND HUMAN DIGNITY

> My religion, what I believe in, is called
> the Constitution of the United States of America.
> —Stephen Meyers, *Ides of March*,
> directed by George Clooney

"WHAT DO YOU have to do with us, Son of God?"[1] This alarming, apocalyptic phrase was pronounced by the two demon-possessed men in Gergesa, the country of the Gergesenes, on the eastern (Golan Heights) side of the Sea of Galilee (the modern name is Khersa), on a day when Jesus came uninvited from Capernaum to their country. This striking phrase could be translated something like: "Leave us alone! You mind your work, and we shall mind our work!" Two separate areas now exist as the result of a process of division within creation: secular and sacred. Our culture has allowed itself to be dominated by a political dualism, with the social and political organized in such a way that almost everyone says that the Church should not interfere with what concerns the world. It seems that invent-

---

[1] Mt 8.29.

ing and promoting the question (and mindset), "What have we to do with you, Son of God?" is actually a method used by the evil one that allows evil to survive and have influence over the world.

That being the case, it is rare to see an Orthodox Christian dealing with the subject of politics in an inclusive and comprehensive way. It is taken for granted that politics has to do with the secularized (legal) protection of human rights (a product of the philosophy of the Enlightenment), within the political system of so-called "representative democracy," which is limited mostly to social utility or to the conventional rules of human relations.[2]

Today's "commercialization of politics—its use of propaganda and publicity with its seeming goal of brainwashing of the masses—has literally abolished the 'representative' parliamentary system."[3] Moral views, divorced from spiritual beliefs, prove to be more disagreeable and pointless to contemporary man than ever before. So why bother with politics when every citizen of so-called developed societies has a direct, according to Yannaras's perspective, everyday experience of the rapid decline and alienation of the fundamental aspects of modernity?

Most Christians look at politics and democracy as unrelated to their experience of the Church itself, which both abides in history and expects the Kingdom, the eschaton. We should remember, however, that the postponement of the Kingdom is the devil's goal. When the demons say, "Have you come here to torment us *before the time*?"[4] they are saying that they want him to come later. Anyone who is dominated in his or her interest by historical concerns prays for the Kingdom to

[2]Cf. Christos Yannaras, *The Meaning of Reality: Essays on Existence and Communion, Eros and History* (Los Angeles: Sebastian Press, 2011), 150.

[3]Yannaras, *The Meaning of Reality*, 49.

[4]Mt 8.29.

not come too quickly. One who idealizes history and politics is also abolishing the eschaton from his or her mind and heart.

How are we to make sense of this? First, we keep in mind that this hermeneutical perspective does not avoid political concerns. The image of the Church is a *polis*, "the holy city, new Jerusalem, which descends from heaven,"[5] which is a communion of persons living in this world. "The political theory of the Church is the truth of the Holy Trinity," as Fedorov used to say.[6] This truth is not some distant metaphysical principle, nor is it given as an intellectual idea. It is an *incarnation* in history; it is the person of the incarnate Word-Christ, who in the communion of the Spirit reveals the will of the Father. This is to be found in the experience of the Church, understood as a holistic manifestation of the love of God, which in a very personal way, as an outburst amidst the stillness, evaporates the deceptiveness of political delusions, granting the truth of life as an *ecclesial* blessing of freedom and unity. In the words of Brandon Gallaher, the Orthodox worldview holds that "religion is not privatized but speaks to the minutiae of life including the ordering of society which in every part is called to transfiguration and thereby secularism in its popular sense of a 'neutral sphere' is a lie."[7]

Politikon Zōon and Zōon Theoumenon

By *nature*, human animals are political animals, according to Aristotle.[8] To address the human as political animal is to accentuate his

---

[5]Rev 21.2.

[6]See in Yannaras, *The Meaning of Reality*, 151.

[7]Brandon Gallaher, "The Orthodox Moment: The Holy and Great Council in Crete and Orthodoxy's Encounter with the West: On Learning to Love the Church," *Sobornost* 39.2 (2017): 46.

[8]"Man is by nature a political animal (πολιτικὸν ζῷον) . . . man is not only a politi-

horizontal element: his bond, as a human, with the others of his kind. From this spring the universal and inalienable natural human *rights*, which are not dependent on the laws or customs of any particular culture or government. However, as Kallistos Ware holds, this horizontal dimension must be complemented by the vertical axis: "our relationship with God." According to Ware, "it is this characteristic of human personhood to which St Gregory of Nazianzus (+c.390) draws attention when he describes the human being not as *politikon zōon* but as *zōon theoumenon*, 'an animal that is being deified.' (*Oration 38*, 11)."[9] Therefore, our right to become gods (the right of deification) is the right of *personhood* and does not belong to the realm of so-called natural rights.[10]

The implications of this feature of human personhood for our picture of politics are a subject of ongoing research. Indeed, people have rights both as individuals (natural and legal rights) and as persons. So, there are rights that are human (like the right of deification), and yet are neither legal nor natural. Still, one issue has to be settled, namely to reconcile the law of personhood with the law of the individual. Zizioulas persuasively argued that "the law of personhood is not based either on natural law or on the conventional and essentially utilitarian necessities of a social organization, but on an ontology of relations without which nothing could exist as free, not even God Himself."[11] Most theologians attempt to explain this distinction in the following way:

cal but a social animal (κοινωνικὸν ζῷον ὁ ἄνθρωπος)." Aristotle, *Politics* 1.1252a24–1253a8 (trans. Barnes).

[9] Bishop Kallistos Ware, "Who is Man?" *Again Magazine* 20, no. 4 (1997/98): 27–31, cited in http://www.antiochian.org/Orthodox_Church_Who_What_Where_Why/ Who_Is_Man.htm. Accessed May 2, 2017. Kallistos also adds, "Made in God's image, as humans we are capable of sharing in the divine life, of becoming "partakers of the divine nature (2 Pet 1.4)."

[10] Cf. Perišić, *Theological Disambiguations*, 249–59.

[11] Zizioulas, *The One and the Many*, 405.

"As individuals people have the rights which come from their nature and which, by intention, protect them (as individuals) from the state and society."[12] These are "human rights" in the conventional sense of "natural rights." However, as *persons*, people have the exclusive right to achieve *deification*, "if possible, in the state and thanks to the state, and if not possible, then outside it and even in spite of it, and also in spite of their own nature."[13]

For this reason, in the current political climate it is useful and necessary to overcome the manifest individualism and a culture of "rights," which leads to the subjective alteration of rights into entitlements for happiness, as discussed in the Encyclical of the Holy and Great Council of Crete in 2016.[14] The present political understanding—as a response to contemporary social and political crises and upheavals—is limited to protecting the freedom of the individual but not of the person.

> The approach to human rights on the part of the Orthodox Church centers on the danger of individual rights falling into individualism and a culture of "rights." A perversion of this kind functions at the expense of the social content of freedom and leads to the arbitrary transformation of rights into claims for happiness, as well as the elevation of the precarious identification of freedom with individual license into a "universal value" that undermines the foundations of social values, of the family, of religion, of the nation and threatens fundamental moral values.[15]

[12]See, for example, Perišić, *Theological Disambiguations*, 254.

[13]Ibid., 255.

[14]"Encyclical of the Holy and Great Council of the Orthodox Church," *Annual 2016 of the Western American Diocese* (Los Angeles: Sebastian Press, 2016), 32–40.

[15]"Encyclical of the Holy and Great Council of the Orthodox Church," *Annual 2016 of the Western American Diocese* (Los Angeles: Sebastian Press, 2016), 38.

Yannaras has highlighted the conception of the social and political event that is borne by the Orthodox ecclesiastical tradition, which entails a *personalistic* (in that it assumes the human person to be of infinite value, as opposed to Western utilitarian individualism) and *relational* approach. Yannaras goes on to say:

> The Greek *mode* was embodied historically in the *common struggle for truth* that is *political* life, the art and science of politics, the realization of the *polis* and of *democracy* as an existential (not utilitarian) goal. The Western *mode* was embodied in the safeguarding of the individual with *rights* guaranteed by institutions and conventions, as well as in amazingly advanced technological means of satisfying the human urges for self-preservation, domination, and pleasure.[16]

Perhaps this approach may sound artificially dualistic. But, to my mind, the whole problem of the so-called Western mentality lies in the *hermeneutics*. We do not assume that the entire West is individualistic, but that in the West the person is *understood* as an *individual*. Thus, a history written by a Westerner is usually *interpreted* individualistically.[17] A personalistic and relational approach like the Greek mode described by Yannaras requires a faithful engagement with the traditions, all in conversation with political science and philosophy. A theologian, rooted in the catholic being of the Orthodox Church, must offer a methodology that encompasses the abovementioned concerns

[16]Christos Yannaras, *The Schism in Philosophy: The Hellenic Perspective and Its Western Reversal* (Brookline, MA: Holy Cross Orthodox Press, 2015), xiii.

[17]According to Gallaher, "at the West's core is a vision of *individual reason as an abstract power* that posits that which is (Being) before it as an object for its inquiring and relentless gaze, stripping that which is thought down to its essentials, to each of its distinct prts that are known with all the mystery and dark depths eliminated by the clear light of rationality." Gallaher, "The Orthodox Moment," 44.

and transcends moralism. By simply appealing to ethics or rationality, we do not necessarily make people better.

Authority Exercised Tyrannically?

One underlying concern in this discussion of politics lies in the fact that every political system operates with *force* (though not necessarily torture), something that can never become an instrument of the Church, because it *does not make you free.* So we all might agree that any use of metaphysics for political aims—whether enforced or free— transforms metaphysics into a political ideology and psychological illusion. "The truth," we are informed, "shall make you free."[18] In this sense, there is an imperative: "let the greatest among you become as the youngest, and the leader as one who serves."[19]

As we can see, freedom is a tricky issue in politics. No doubt, in America, "since our nations's founding, we have wrestled with what it means to be free."[20] But politics—which continually speaks about human rights and human dignity—is indifferent to the supposed freedom of the human *person.* The organizational structures of corporate life do not allow for an emergence of personal distinctiveness and freedom.[21] For this reason, the Cretan Council of 2016 emphasizes that the Orthodox understanding of man

> is opposed both to the arrogant apotheosis of the individual and his rights, and to the humiliating debasement of the human person

[18]Jn 8.32.

[19]Lk 22.25–26.

[20]Nat Hentoff, foreword to *First Freedoms: A Documentary History of First Amendment Rights in America*, ed. C. C. Haynes, S. Chaltrain, and S. M. Glison (Oxford: Oxford University Press, 2006), 10.

[21]Cf. Christos Yannaras, *The Freedom of Morality*, trans. Elizabeth Briere (Crestwood, NY: St Vladimir's Seminary Press, 1984), 225.

within the vast contemporary structures of economy, society, politics and communication. . . . No one has honored man and cared for him as much as the God-man Christ and his Church. A fundamental human right is the protection of the principle of religious freedom in all its aspects—namely, the freedom of conscience, belief, and religion, including, alone and in community, in private and in public, the right to freedom of worship and practice, the right to manifest one's religion, as well as the right of religious communities to religious education and to the full function and exercise of their religious duties, without any form of direct or indirect interference by the state.[22]

You might ask why Christ assumed that political authority is exercised tyrannically[23] and that the power of those who dominate others is oppressive and provisional, while Christ's authority is free and lasting because he was sacrificed to save others. To open our eyes to the true nature of how politics should be, Christ gives this example: "You know that those who are supposed to rule over the Gentiles lord it over them, and their great men exercise authority over them. But it shall not be so among you; but whoever would be great among you must be your servant, and whoever would be first among you must be slave of all."[24] It seems that the "new creation" inaugurated by Christ overthrows the established order. This idea is strongly suggested when one considers several aspects of the common experience. Every form of authority has its rationale in the need for society to function properly and be capable of making effective decisions. Accordingly, every exercise of authority has in the first place the character of an office; it is respected by everybody as a ministry, and whoever is in a position of authority

[22]"Encyclical of the Holy and Great Council," 38.
[23]Cf. Mk 10.42–44.
[24]Mk 10.42–44.

serves the common good. Unfortunately, the exercise of authority in modern politics often manifests characteristics diametrically opposed to those we suppose to belong to its original purpose.

Although the Orthodox may have a certain advantage in not going entirely through the well-known "Western paradigm,"[25] they are nonetheless forced to face the postmodern paradigm shift in the West. As the Holy and Great Council of 2016 clearly stated:

> The Church does not involve herself with politics in the narrow sense of the term. Her witness, however, is essentially political insofar as it expresses concern for man and his spiritual freedom. The voice of the Church was always distinct and will ever remain a beneficial intervention for the sake of humanity.[26]

In discussing ethical dilemmas in the fields of politics, medicine, biology, or technology, many ask if *ethical* dilemmas have any relation to the metaphysical meaning of human existence. However, people do not adopt a political viewpoint because such a thing is rational or moral. The present problem is critical because the moral relativism and individualism that undergird the social education of our time have imposed upon us social and psychological conditions that tend to dissolve the integrity of our personal being into ontically separate individualities and personalities alienated from communion and relation, so that the human being's irreplaceable and unique personhood, which only flowers in true communion and the call to relation, becomes lost. At the beginning of the twenty-first century, the networks of economic

---

[25]We have to admit that, mainly due to historical reasons, the Orthodox world did not organically participate in the phenomenon of modernity, the Renaissance, the Reformation or the Counter-Reformation, European Wars of Religion, the Enlightenment, the French and the Industrial Revolutions, Romanticism, Modernity, Postmodernity, the ascent of the subject, human rights, a religiously neutral nation state, etc., etc.

[26]"Encyclical of the Holy and Great Council," 38.

and political interests in the international sphere have led to a social corruption that increases dramatically through the immorality of the media and their focus on ratings, sponsors, sensationalism, and propaganda rather than truth. Regrettably, the media's presentation of events often comes at the expense of providing viewers with the truth.

"Render to Caesar the Things That Are Caesar's"

The confusion caused by modernity is not limited to the Orthodox world but is also present on a global scale. This offers a theoretical conundrum, to which the Orthodox have yet to address a new prophetic call to a dialogical theology.

> The local Orthodox Churches are today called to promote a new constructive synergy with the secular state and its rule of law within the new framework of international relations, in accordance with the biblical saying: "Render to Caesar the things that are Caesar's and to God the things that are God's" (cf. Mt 22.21).[27]

A communion-centered version of society, based on the protection of human existential truth and authenticity, might produce a *new* cultural paradigm able to translate *theōsis* into politics. The consensus among Orthodox theologians is that synergy with the secular state "must, however, preserve the specific identity of both Church and state and ensure their earnest cooperation in order to preserve man's unique dignity and the human rights which flow therefrom, and in order to assure social justice."[28]

Man cannot be nourished with "husks,"[29] nor only by "antidoron." You cannot participate without the political responsibility of belonging,

[27]Ibid.
[28]Ibid.
[29]See Lk 15.16.

and only through the proxy of representation. Any kind of eucharistic "decaffeination" (docetism) leads to political and cultural "decaffeination." So, maybe only a restoration of the parish or the diocese could serve as a *political* program.[30] Recently, Aristotle Papanikolaou published a book, *The Mystical as Political*, in which he argues that "a eucharistic ecclesiology that integrates the ascetical tradition leads to an endorsement of the principles of modern liberal democracy, and that such an endorsement is not a betrayal of the ecclesial vision of the world being created for communion with God."[31] This thesis is profound but not easily applied because of one simple question: can the ecclesiastical tradition adopt the idea of collectivism as a *society* blending together individuals in the pursuit of common interests? If the ecclesial tradition, according to Yannaras, is incompatible with collectivism as an arithmetic sum total of nondifferentiated individuals, then how can an Orthodox Christian lead an active public life in Western society if he or she is not fully conscious of the basic worldview of the Church?

Two Political Worldviews

A few decades ago, the president of a world superpower visited an Orthodox country and was asked in a TV interview how his belief in God affected his political views and actions. He replied that he and his whole family believe in the Ten Commandments. That was all. The

---

[30]Or, according to Sotiris Mitralexis, "The only *radical* political program capable of effecting *actual*, civilization-wide change, in which the ecclesial event engenders a bottom-up political theology simply by the fact that it is realized" ("The Eucharistic Community is Our Social Program: On the Early Development of Christos Yannaras' Political Theology," *Political Theology*, published November 28, 2017, https://doi.org/10.1080/1462317X.2017.1402550, 13).

[31]Aristotle Papanikolaou, *The Mystical as Political: Democracy and Non-Radical Orthodoxy* (Notre Dame, IN: Notre Dame University Press, 2012), 56.

country he visited was one in which, centuries ago, a pious Orthodox emperor had written a hymn: "Come, all peoples, let us worship
the Godhead in three persons: the Son in the Father, with the Holy
Spirit. For the Father begat the Son before all ages, co-eternal and
equal in majesty, and the Holy Spirit was in the Father, glorified with
the Son: a single power, a single essence, one Godhead, which we all
worship. . . ."[32] The difference between the two approaches is obvious
(two "cosmocrators" with different levels of philosophy), but this only
illuminates a puzzling question: why is theology today so divorced
from politics?

History has known two modes of organizing life, or two cultural-
civilizational paradigms: communion-centric (which marks Greco-
Roman and European thought from ancient Athens: the Hellenic
polis and Christian society, mostly in the East) and individual-centric
(initially barbarian and then modern—mostly Western) ways of life.
Since history cannot go backward and is unable to merely imitate the
past, can we (as modern men and women) find *a third paradigm* for
our human history and society? One that is a mode of organizing life,
going beyond utilitarianism and individualism, and reaching the *evan-
gelion* as the *tropos* that saves our mortal existence and leads us to the
mode of Uncreated, or *tertium non datur*?

The relevance of this question and these observations is limited,
however, since ours is a postmodern, not a classical, society. In modern
society with our real-world politics, there are resemblances to this classical perspective; there are also potentially pivotal differences.

---

[32]From the great vespers of Pentecost, Aposticha, eighth tone. The author of the
hymn is the Emperor Leo VI the Wise (886–912), who is depicted above the Central
Royal Doors of Hagia Sophia in Constantinople, in a posture of deep repentance, in
adoration, barely raising his hands and face from the ground, a poor suppliant before
his Lord, Christ Enthroned.

To put it simply, society is composed of individuals (atoms who pursue their own interests) or of distinct groups, all of them with their own identity and necessities. The political practice has the goal of discovering a *modus vivendi*: the expression of individual antagonism has to be restricted by or guided through institutions, so as to avoid *bellum omnium contra omnes*, or the war of all against all. Obedience to process is thus the core of a modern democratic society: one has to follow the accepted rules of the game and to succumb to the result of the process.[33]

Eschatologically Conditioned Politics?

The status of freedom and its role within fundamental political law remain unresolved. What should be done? The Orthodox Church evidently has to deal with this reality having itself no political or economic power. The Church's worldly weakness today even puts into question its very survival in the third millennium. And yet, this exact period of history invites institutions to be reconstituted, since no establishment can be taken for granted as a historical necessity. This has tremendous political implications. Any new paradigm that is to be created needs not only new interpretations and criteria but also a new conception of

[33]Cf. Peter Van Nuffelen, who points out some of the oddities of modern democracies: "A US president who is elected with barely 52 percent of the votes is hailed as having received a powerful mandate from the population, and he is allowed to rule against the will of the other 48 percent. A president elected with less votes in absolute numbers than his opponent is still legally elected because the procedure prescribes the existence of an electoral college. Even more puzzling, from a pre-modern perspective, is that in the UK, between 2005 and 2010, a party with just 35% of the vote was able to govern the country. Elections in modern democracies are thus not tools to generate consensus but to adjudicate profound disagreement" (Peter Van Nuffelen, "The Rhetoric of Rules and the Rule of Consensus," in *Episcopal Elections in Late Antiquity*, ed. Johan Leemans, Peter Van Nuffelen, Shawn Keoughe, and Carla Nicolaye [Berlin: De Gruyter, 2011], 250).

politics—different from the one that is found at the heart of Western European civilization. In the constructing of such a new paradigm, Orthodoxy would have as its tools an eschatologically conditioned history. What does that mean? If the Church offers its eschatological *ethos* to the new paradigm, then a new political theory and action can emerge that will not be limited merely to social utility or to the conventional rules of human relations, even if these are more "efficient." This new ethos presupposes deeply existential—and not simply "rational" or "moral"—motivations in order to function. Its goal might be the truth of man and the authenticity of his existence.

Remarkably, one of the main characteristics of contemporary Orthodox theology is its faithfulness to the Tradition understood both as continuity with the past and as something avant-garde. In fact, as John Milbank argues eloquently, "the pathos of modern theology is its false humility. For theology, this must be a fatal disease, because once theology surrenders its claim to be a meta-discourse, it cannot any longer articulate the word of the creator God, but is bound to turn into the oracular voice of some finite idol, such as historical scholarship, humanist psychology, or transcendental philosophy."[34] In spite of many differences, almost everyone agrees that preserving the Tradition is just one aspect of being Orthodox and that an engagement with its interpretation in the light of today's and tomorrow's basic existential concerns is imperative. Thus, as Milbank contends, "if theology no longer seeks to position, qualify or criticize other discourses, then it is inevitable that these discourses will position theology: for the necessity of an ultimate organizing logic cannot be wished away."[35]

In the winter of 371, the Roman emperor Valens, who was mercilessly sending into exile any bishop who displeased him, suddenly

---

[34]John Milbank, *Theology and Social Theory* (Malden, MA: Blackwell, 1990), 1.
[35]Ibid.

appeared in Cappadocia. He sent the prefect Modestus to Archbishop Basil, and Modestus began to threaten the saint with the confiscation of his property, banishment, beatings, and even death. In a dialogue with deepest political connotations, St Basil invoked the basic human right with a sentence that summarizes his anthropology: "I am God's creation commanded to become god."[36]

Ultimately, following St Basil the Great, we must understand how important it is to be courageous in dealing with the very sensitive issue of the relationship between the Church and society, especially with regard to urgent contemporary political and socioeconomic issues. As a free Church in a free society, the Church has the right to ask of a state: (a) *to protect its freedom and identity* (whenever it is threatened by other social or religious groups), (b) *not to enforce laws that impose the violation of the principles of its members in the public life* (or to guarantee their rights against the autonomy of the states), and (c) *not to intervene in its internal affairs.* However, one should be aware that this cannot be done without *theological* criteria, that is, this can be done only through the *relational experience of the Church* and politics grounded on the quest for *meaning.* Only this can balance the relationship between the Church and state.

Readily listening to global ecumenical theological conversations and following the best theological voices from East and West, a theologian must focus on a *personalistic* rather than an individualistic view of the law and politics. The logic is simple. If, as a politician or technician within the fields of science or administration in modern society, an Orthodox Christian does not transmit the Orthodox vision, he will then himself be assimilated to the very mentality he is called upon

---

[36]Θεοῦ τε κτίσμα ὑπάρχων, καὶ θεός εἶναι κεκελευσμένος. The entire dialogue is described by St Gregory the Theologian in his *Funeral Oration for Basil the Great* 48.4.

to change. How can an Orthodox woman or man be a minister of culture if that person is not conscious of the aesthetic and eucharistic approach to human creation, and would act merely according to goal-oriented criteria and utilitarian approaches?[37]

In conclusion, the Orthodox Church, being true to an authentic theology of incarnation inspired by the experience of the Resurrection, and having adopted the audacity of the Holy Fathers, has to enter into a dialogue and produce a new synthesis with that which is best in the modern world. If the Orthodox man or woman wishes to transmit to Western society what it lacks, and which is amply offered by Orthodoxy, then he or she must reconcile the law of personhood with the law of the individual.

Law, politics, and the Church are obliged to work together in affirming both individual and personal rights. Only then the *icon* of God,[38] that is, the person of man, shall be preserved from the dangers that threaten it. Both in the ecclesial and political arenas, *politikon zōon and zōon theoumenon* must be equally honored.

---

[37]Cf. J. Zizioulas, Ὀρθοδοξία καὶ σύγχρονος κόσμος [Orthodoxy and the Modern World] (Nicosia, 2006).

[38]Cf. Alfons Brüning, "Orthodox Theology in Dialogue with Human Rights: Some Considerations on Current Themes, Problems, and Perspectives," *Exchange* 45 (2016): 390: "This Orthodox point of view generates a more dynamic understanding of 'Human Dignity' in comparison with the static opinions prevailing in the West (in both secular and theological approaches): In rough terms, the 'image of God' in this understanding is not just an immutable essence, that could more or less easily be equated with 'Human Dignity' also in a non-religious perception, but rather a potential that needs yet to be unfolded and developed."

Synodality:
A Misapprehended Vision

AT THE Council of Nicaea in 325, the so-called Meletian schism was resolved in such a way that the council Fathers received into communion the prior schismatic Meletius of Lycopolis without requiring him to be reconsecrated, thereby also accepting all of his consecrated bishops and presbyters. Through some surprising logic, the Church accepted all of the baptisms, consecrations, and mysteries performed by these schismatics (and in other cases of heretical Arians)—which were, understandably, meaningless and invalid at the time of their performance—*retroactively* and conciliarily, recognizing them as valid after they had repented. This is not the only example of this happening in the history of the Church,[1] but it brings us to the logical question: how could the Fathers of the council possibly perform this intervention into the past and "correct" it? Or, in other words, how can decisions be made about the past from the perspective of the future? Is this simply the work of the Church's *oikonomia*, or is it a general psychological state where some individual rewrites and reinterprets his or her past? Or is it perhaps the well-established legal principle of retroactive force of law?

The answer given by Church Tradition states that this is neither a psychological nor a legal theme but rather something related to ontology, because it involves an existential question about the very being of

[1]Cf. Canon 1 of St Basil the Great.

concrete persons as members of the Church assembly (body). Thus, it is a question of decisions of an ontological nature, addressing the ecclesial existence of those who were ecclesiologically (even if only for a while) nonexistent. This sort of action demonstrates that the mentioned person(s) did retroactively exist within the salvific milieu of the Church.[2] The above example—which should be kept in mind as we explore authority and primacy—reminds us of the theological truth that the Omega (or eschaton) is its own kind of Alpha ("*archē*," or beginning, hypostasis) of the Church and its praxis, a beginning that constitutes the Church, giving it identity, survival, and inspiration. Still, this is indeed one of many surprising paradoxes that we encounter today in theological science.

The convocation of the Holy and Great Council of the Orthodox Church in 2016 has aroused curiosity about the vital importance of the structure of the Church. This large-scale synodal event has invited the Churches to reconsider the question of synodality and the thorny question of primacy, free from a millennium-old prejudice.

However, in our day, the large-scale synodal events of the Church of the first millennium are either forgotten or misapprehended or both. In recent times, these events seem to be accompanied, on most occasions, by a polemic that psychologically loads the debate concerning the issue at hand. Thus, the Holy and Great Council in Crete was wrongly interpreted in some circles, and today we see that whenever

---

[2]The Council of Nicaea in 325 attempted to create peace with the Meletians. Meletius had nominated bishops without the concurrence of the other bishops of the province, and without the approval of the metropolitan of Alexandria, and had thus occasioned a schism. He was allowed to remain bishop of Lycopolis, but without the right to ordain bishops outside his region. The bishops he had already ordained were accepted under certain restrictions, and some had to be reordained. See Henry R. Percival, *The Seven Ecumenical Councils of the Undivided Church*, vol. 14 of *The Nicene and Post-Nicene Fathers*, Series 2, ed. Philip Schaff and Henry Wace (1900; repr., Peabody, MA: Hendrickson, 1994).

and however it is referred to, some people make it the target of public *odium*.

There are different angles from which to approach the topic of synodality. I hope here to point the way to a more nuanced and realistic understanding of how councils took place and the role played by the episcopacy in them.[3] Within the scope of this article, I would like to explore the significance of "synodality" when one sees it as a portrayal of Pentecost and an expression of the Liturgy. However, in order to reach that vision, I will have to, for the most part, limit myself to the more forthright aspects, since synodality is not only "forgotten" in our day but also misinterpreted. So, let us look within Church history for examples from the period of the early local and ecumenical councils.

Misapprehended Synodality

Should someone randomly ask people on the street what, in their opinion, "synodality" is about, the reply he or she will hear as a rule (if the person being questioned knows what synodality is to begin with) is the following: a synod is an old-fashioned "institution" detached from ordinary people, a governance dealing with administrative affairs, advocating the church's laws and morals—in short, something out of touch with the reality of most people. Occasionally, someone may note that a synod usually includes "collegiality," which means that a synod is governed in a collegial fashion so that its head exercises his authority in a more circumspect fashion.

[3] The councils, as a rule, bring hope. The iconography of the councils depends on the iconography of Pentecost, which was a council *sui generis*. The choreography in these icons demonstrates colorfully that the Church understood these councils as eucharistic events—in the image of Pentecost and the Apocalypse. It is interesting to observe that Salvador Dalí painted a surreal painting *The Ecumenical Council* (1960, kept in Dalí's museum in St Petersburg in Florida), one of his masterpieces, as an expression of his renewed hope in religious leadership after the disastrous World War II.

The meaning of synodality in most people's minds appears to be linked to static, legalistic, and formal criteria. The more legalistic a synod is, the more "true" it is. And the more *conservative* the conciliar fathers are, displaying spiritual authority, special gifts, and so forth, the more this induces us to regard them as "holy fathers." The same applies reversely: when we discern a certain weakness in a council (such as the absence of some churches, procedural deficiencies, presence of the non-Orthodox, etc.), then we tend to mentally mark it off the "holy councils" list.

This common and widespread perception of synodality gives rise to certain basic questions when placed under the light of our Tradition. Let us mention some of them:

1. If synodality is mainly about observing legal and moral values—as some claim—then why did the Apostolic Synod introduce an innovation regarding the Jewish law and accept the universal mission of the Church? We usually call the Apostolic Synod a "*sui generis council,*" but it was, in fact, the foundation of all future innovation in ecclesial life (such as the Councils of Nicaea I [325] and II [787], Chalcedon [451], Constantinople I [381] and II [553], etc.). The apostles were not hesitant to get together and—"after there had been much debate" (πολλῆς ζητήσεως γενομένης, Acts 15.7)—they innovated regarding the most pressing issues of their time.[4]

2. There is a group of theologians who see little, if any, connection between conciliarity and the Liturgy of the Church. The separation of these two aspects of ecclesiology through the practice of having councils outside the liturgical context has resulted in several distortions of synodality that contradict fundamental principles of ecclesiology.

[4]This openness was a foundation for any other attempt in approaching the world, and it led St Gregory the Theologian to affirm the principle of "coining new terms": εἰ δεῖ τι καὶ καινοτομῆσαι περὶ τὰ ὀνόματα σαφηνείας ἕνεκεν (*Oration* 39.12 [PG 36:348B]).

But the Liturgy itself was never entirely divorced from conciliarity.[5] At a time when the term "synod" had become a *terminus technicus* for the formal councils, people used it *also* for the Liturgy.[6] On the other hand, the word "*synodos*" is used by the Holy Fathers (such as Sts John Chrysostom, Cyril of Alexandria, Gregory the Theologian, Cyril of Alexandria, Proclus of Constantinople, Maximus the Confessor, and others) to describe an aspect of the Christological issue. (They used the word "synod" to describe the unity between the two natures in Christ.) Therefore, the history of synodality indicates that the goal of the Church councils was never a formulation of faith per se, but the confirmation of eucharistic communion (κοινωνία), as reconciliation between the "other" (a Christlike person) and "others" (eucharistic communities). The main theme of the canons has therefore always been the restoration to full communion of those excommunicated (τῶν ἀκοινωνήτων).[7]

3. A similar difficulty results from the principle that "*each and every bishop must participate at a council*," which is advocated by many. This axiom is repeated by many who imply that the Holy and Great Council was deficient because all bishops were not present.[8] Along those lines,

[5] As shown by the study by Nicholas Denysenko, "Synodality and the Rite of Ordination of a Bishop," in *Synodality: A Forgotten and Misapprehended Vision: Reflections on the Holy and Great Council 2016*, eds. Maxim Vasiljević and Andrej Jeftić (Los Angeles: Sebastian Press, 2017), 69–80.

[6] See, e.g., St John Chrysostom, *De Proph. obsc.* 2.5 (PG 56:182). Also St Jerome, *Epist. ad Heliodorum* 12 (PL 22:597). Cf. Zizioulas, *One and the Many*, 208.

[7] Canon 5 of the First Ecumenical Council is but one of countless examples. More about this in John Zizioulas, "Ὁ Συνοδικὸς Θεσμός: Ἱστορικά, Ἐκκλησιαστικὰ καὶ Κανονικὰ Προβλήματα," in *Τιμητικὸν Ἀφιέρωμα εἰς τὸν Μητροπολίτην Κίτρους Βαρνάβαν ἐπὶ τῇ 25ετηρίδι τῆς Ἀρχιερατείας του* ["The Institution of the Synod: Historical, Ecclesiological, and Canonical Problems," Festschrift to Metropolitan of Kitros Varnavas] (Athens, 1980), 169.

[8] Cf. Met. Hierotheos Vlachos: "Only a select few bishops were allowed to attend–not invited. Because the entire college of bishops were not invited then it implies

it's interesting to note that although at the First Ecumenical Council, presumably, there existed a direct relation of the local church with the council, the subsequent councils introduced a form of *representation* of church-administrative regions. It is said that at the great councils all bishops must attend, as if this were the canonical criterion of the councils' "ecumenicity." But this alone is still not proof of true synodality; it is of no value if the prerequisite of *synodal "phronēma"* (consensus) does not exist—in other words, a *"phronēma"* that even a council without numerous bishops can have.[9] At the Fifth Ecumenical Council, interestingly, Pope Vigilius requested the metropolitan system (that is, a system that accommodated the geographical criterion) while the Eastern bishops insisted on *representations of equal number from all five patriarchal thrones*.[10] Therefore, if we accept the thesis that all churches and all bishops must participate in a Holy and Great Council, then we must also take issue with the practice of the Seven Ecumenical Councils, of which the Seventh introduced new canonical criteria for a coun-

that they are not equal and hence not real bishops" ("The Decisions of the Hierarchy of the Church of Greece on the 'Holy and Great Council' and Their Fate," trans. Anastasios Filippides, Holy Metropolis of Nafpaktos and Saint Vlasios, posted september 28, 2016, http://parembasis.gr/index.php/holy-great-council-menu/4622-2016-09-ni-decisions-church-of-greece-holy-council-and-their-fate; Greek original: http://parembasis.gr/index.php/el/metropolitan/articles/4618-2016-09-25, accessed April 27, 2018).

[9]As Russian historian Vasili Bolotov pointed out, "For an Ecumenical Council, it is not necessary to have it convened by the pope, nor to have his participation, nor the participation of the individual Churches, nor the momentary recognition as such from the individual Churches. It is necessary that the truth be manifested, which is contained in the entire Ecumenical Church. This point is arrived at only by a long historical process. The Church's life alone in history, not some formal characteristics, puts such a seal on the Councils. This was the case with the following Councils: the Nicene, both Constantinopolitan, the Ephesian and the Chalcedonian" (Vasili Bolotov, *Lectures in the History of Ancient Church* [in Serbian] [Kraljevo, 2010], 271).

[10]See Vlasios J. Pheidas, *The History of the Church*, vol. 1 [in Greek] (Athens, 1994), 878.

cil to be *ecumenical*. These new criteria required that representatives from the seats of Rome and Constantinople must "participate in it," and representatives of the patriarchates—Alexandria, Antioch, and Jerusalem—must be "in agreement," that is, give their explicit consent.[11]

4. Analogous problems also arise when synodality is linked to the "quantitative" aspect, that is, seeking "validation from numbers" (*auctoritas ex numero*).[12] Many people revert to this approach because it is interesting; yet, it is not Orthodox, nor is it accurate. Numbers and synodality do not relate to each other, nor do they necessarily coexist. As Fr John Behr noted, some councils, "such as Ariminium-Seleucia in 359, had more attendants (560) than any ecumenical council."[13] For instance, the episcopal composition of the Second (381) and Third Ecumenical Councils (431) was on the basis of the metropolitan system, while after the Fourth Ecumenical Council it was in accordance with the patriarchical administrative system. Consequently, to say that one "third" of the bishops (from the four absent patriarchates) was not present in Crete is as absurd canonically and historically as it would be to say that at some ecumenical council some "third" was not present. At some of the ecumenical councils a "third" of the Episcopate was indeed absent, while at others there was not even a "third" of the bishops *present*.[14] Still, each of the ecumenical councils was recognized after two years or more.

[11]Cf. J. D. Mansi, *Sacrorum Conciliorum Nova Amplissima Collectio* (Florence, 1795ff), 8:208–9.

[12]See Sulpicius Severus, *Chronicle* 2.33.1.

[13]John Behr, "The Holy and Great Council 2016," in *Synodality: A Forgotten and Misapprehended Vision*, 16.

[14]Regarding the question of the presence of all churches at the Great Ecumenical Councils, we can cite Bolotov, who, in the case of the First Ecumenical Council (about which the unjustifiable and unhistorical thought has been that it was a council of all the bishops), says, "It is assumed with a level of certainty that at that time there were around one thousand dioceses in the East and about eight hundred in the West. Therefore, only one sixth of the Christian bishops were present" (Bolotov, *Lectures*, 271).

5. The next fundamental misunderstanding involves seeing the council as a matter of singularity in the objective arithmetical sense, as a sort of objectified reality per se, as an entity in itself (according to substantialist ontology). Historically, only the postcouncil period demonstrated whether a council measured up to and fulfilled the criterion of the ecumenical councils. A council is conditioned *epicletically* and cannot be communicated in seclusion from the communities, whether through individuals or systems of ideas. To the claim, many times repeated, that the council in Crete was not a "Holy and Great Council" due to certain weaknesses, the Tradition has no other answer than the following: *the future gives meaning and hypostasis to the past.* This makes the council a relational reality. Let us recall the Third Ecumenical Council. St Cyril of Alexandria began and finished this council without the Antiochian Church, which was led by John of Antioch with forty bishops. While St Cyril chaired "his" council, John summoned his own council, in which he condemned St Cyril and his followers. After two years, early in 433, Cyril and the Antiochian bishops agreed on the Formula of Reunion, and "Cyril's council" became the Third Ecumenical Council. Remember, at St Cyril's Third Ecumenical Council in 431 there were thousands of flaws in the proceedings, so much so that Bishop John of Antioch was forced to anathematize St Cyril's council. How, then, is it that this synod is ecumenical when it is clear that its historical manifestation did not conform to the requirements of an "ideal synod"?

6. Most studies on conciliarity presume that a synod must be a "success," in terms of achieving unity and vanquishing heresies. Yet, if we identify synodality with "success"—with the final results in *verbal* and *practical* agreement—then we will need to admit that many councils were not so "successful."[15] We must understand here that a dogmatic

[15] The Fourth and Fifth Ecumenical Councils were not successful in bringing

"gigantomachia" does not simply end in the agreement of words and formulas, but in *the reality of the Mystery*, recognized (sacramentally and liturgically) in the Image of the crucified and resurrected Christ.[16] It is indicative that St Polycarp, the famous bishop of Smyrna, in about the year 155 visited his Roman brother Pope Anicetus to discuss with him the disputed issue of the date of Pascha. Although they did not agree on all things, they nonetheless served the Liturgy together, after which Polycarp returned to Smyrna—to his martyrdom.

7. Many people think that a council should be an "open-ended event" (i.e., unfinished). However, the two-thousand-year-long history of the Church has never included an "open-ended council." Even a series of patriarchal councils, the so-called Hesychast (or Palamite) Councils, held in the Byzantine capital of Constantinople between 1341 and 1351, which dealt with the same topic, consisted of six separate councils, each having its own conclusion and ending session. Canonically, *it is impossible to leave a council "unfinished"* (unless "open" means something else), because that puts into question the *validity* of all the adopted and signed decisions of the council. Here, we should try to think of and clar-

---

about unity in the Church. For more on the aftermath of the Council of Chalcedon in the Holy Land and monks rebelling against Juvenal, Bishop of Jerusalem, see Cornelia B. Horn, *Asceticism and Christological Controversy in Fifth-Century Palestine: The Career of Peter the Iberian* (Oxford: Oxford University Press, 2006). Regarding the Fifth Ecumenical Council, although the Chalcedonian churches did not question its ecumenical status, in the West, the Council of 553 was accepted but not placed on a par with its predecessors. "But hostility to the emperor's programme in Palestine and the west and the indifference of overwhelmingly non-Chalcedonian Egypt made its ecumenicity depend rather too heavily on imperial and (subsequently) papal confirmation." R. Price, *The Acts of the Council of Constantinople of 553: With Related Texts on the Three Chapters Controversy* 2 (Liverpool: Liverpool University Press, 2009), 299.

[16]The Seventh Ecumenical Council "spent relatively little time on the theology of images as such, except where this was relevant in the refutation of the Horos of 754" (Leslie Brubaker and John Haldon, *Byzantium in the Iconoclast Era c. 680–850: A History* [Cambridge: Cambridge University Press, 2011], 284).

ify the *council* as a "court" and an "authority." Many councils served to either confirm or reject a previous council. Never in history was there a condemnation of a heresy that was not confirmed by a council. This is why it is said that a council is the *final* expression of faith. A different practice has simply not been recorded. For instance, no one could annul the "Robber Council" of Ephesus in 449 until a new council was called, in Chalcedon in 451 (a similar relation exists between the Council in Hieria and the Seventh Ecumenical Council).

8. To the list of misapprehensions of synodality one must add the current, widespread trend of promoting an idyllic picture of the councils. Some are ready to speak of the "Church of the Councils." But our Church is not only that; it is also *a conciliar (synodal) Church.* And yet, all councils always had unpredictable, usually distressing moments, and the conciliar acts provide for a broader range of episcopal conduct.[17] Bolotov soberly speaks of them:

> The Second Ecumenical Council in 381 in Constantinople completely met the ideal: neither the emperor was present nor his representatives. This was, in the true sense of the word, a "council of hierarchs." Still, even here things were not completely quiet and peaceful: some of the meetings resembled, to St. Gregory the Theologian, a council of herons.[18]

Needless to say, at all councils the delegates were exposed to enormous psychological pressure.[19] Basically, "each council remained

---

[17]See more in Michael Whitby, "An Unholy Crew? Bishops Behaving Badly at Church Councils," in *Chalcedon in Context: Church Councils 400–700,* Translated Texts for Historians, Contexts 1, ed. Richard Price, Mary Whitby (Liverpool: Liverpool University Press, 2009), 178–96.

[18]Bolotov, *Lectures* [in Serbian], 272.

[19]Among many other things, Hagit Amirav notes "the genuine difficulty in discussing what had been essentially philosophical terminology under circumstances of

unpredictable, despite all due preparations and even pre-drafted scenarios, as it was sometimes the case."[20]

9. Another issue that some people have with the councils is the role (or apparent lack of a role) of the people in them when we talk of a reception that takes place in the living body of the Church.[21] This implies that there should be some sort of "referendum" or "plebiscite." However, the answer to the question "What is the role of the people?" is that the people express themselves through their bishop. The people are not absent, for when the bishop does not rightfully express the views and beliefs of his people, then a new council is called. This was exactly why the council in Florence/Ferrara was rejected—not only by the people, but, more importantly, by the Council of 1484.

10. Another recent suggestion was that it might be more accurate for the Orthodox to say that we are not able to have an ecumenical council today in the model of early Christendom, not because we don't have an emperor to call it (because it can be, and was, called "consensually"), but "because we don't have a Pope who wouldn't be there."[22] However, in the first millennium there were attempts to have the pope at the councils. On December 25, 449, Pope Leo besought Emperor Theodosius to summon an episcopal council in Italy, since this was the

turmoil" (Hagit Amirav, *Authority and Performance Sociological Perspectives on the Council of Chalcedon (AD 451)* [Gottingen: Vandenhoeck & Ruprecht, 2015], 138).

[20]Cyril Hovorun, *Conciliarity and the Holy and Great Council*, in *Synodality: A Forgotten and Misapprehended Vision*, 88.

[21]Indeed, the final decisions of such an institution as a Council "must be tested through their reception by the communities before they can claim full and true authority. Like everything else in an ecclesiology of communion, authority must be *relational*" (Zizioulas, *One and the Many*, 56).

[22]John Behr, "Communion and Conciliarity," the Sir Daniel and Countess Bernardine Murphy Donohue Lecture, February 24, 2011, published in *Album accademico 2010–2011: Pontificio Istituto Orientale*, ed. Edward G. Farrugia (Rome: Pontificio Istituto Orientale, 2011), 48–59.

only sure means of checking the disorder affecting the whole Church, and of preserving the integrity of the catholic faith.[23]

With these insights in mind, we can now pose the question: what is the true nature of a synod? If we wish to say that synodality is possible as a theological and ecclesial reality, then we must seek its meaning beyond legalistic perfection and institutional validity.

Let us see, then, how our Church perceives synodality.

Ecclesial Synodality

1. The Hellenic word σύνοδος (*synodos*, council) has an interesting history. It was popular in classical antiquity, and frequently occurs in the works of such authors as Euripides, Aristophanes, Xenophon, Plato, Aristotle, Epicurus, and others. Ἐκκλησία and σύνοδος were similar public phenomena. The deeper significance of the word σύνοδος is found in St John Chrysostom. In order to emphatically stress his belief in the conciliar nature of the Church, this holy father identified the Church with the synod (ἐκκλησία γὰρ συνόδου ἐστὶν ὄνομα—*Commentary on Psalm 149* 1). Thus, in the ancient Church, from synodality as a political phenomenon, we are led to synodality as a theological one. The Church goes beyond the political meaning that we observe in the ancient Hellenes and Romans (applied to forums, elected representatives, the republic, decision-making in the senate, etc.), and it links the notion of "synod" to eucharistic judgment—something that eventually leads the Holy Fathers to link the term "synod" to Christ himself or the Holy Trinity—that is, to theology.[24]

---

[23]St Leo the Great, *Epistle* 54. Cf. R.V. Sellers, *The Council of Chalcedon: A Historical and Doctrinal Study* (London: SPCK London, 1953), 92. Early in the following year, the emperor requested that a synod should meet under the presidency of the pope in Italy, and that the dispute be brought to an end.

[24]"This interpolation of paschal and eucharistic imagery into the description of

2. Consequently, for the Church, "synodality" relates to Christ and the Holy Spirit and not to any democratic procedure, as in the ancient Greco-Roman world; it became an event, and, in fact, in the Fathers of the Church it is linked to the Pentecost. (It is especially significant that Byzantine iconography depicts the councils as being in the image of Pentecost.)[25] For the Christian faith, synodality (or conciliarity) is therefore not human-centered, but Christ-centered, and is not dependent on the judicial achievements of an institution—great though they may be—but on "the grace of our Lord Jesus Christ, and the love of God the Father, and the communion of the Holy Spirit." It is for this reason that the council is called "*hagia synodos*" (*holy* council): not on account of its virtues, but because it is related to the most holy God.[26]

3. For the Church, synodality is not the individual affirmation of any person, no matter how "saintly" one may be in his or her lifetime; it has to do with the conciliar celebration of the Church. Synodal identity is entirely lost if isolated, for its ontological condition is relationship. It should be noted that, in the case of many ecumenical councils, none of the bishops was invited individually,[27] since only a certain number of them were *invited through their regional metropolitans or exarchs.* On the other hand, none of the ecumenical councils had the right to

the 'conciliar' function of the local Church reveals that not only the context but the ultimate purpose of this function as well is to be found in the eucharistic communion of the Church" (John D. Zizioulas, *The One and the Many: Studies on God, Man, the Church, and the World Today* [Los Angeles: Sebastian Press, 2010], 192).

[25]See my "Reflections on Authority and Synodality: A Eucharistic, Relational, and Eschatological Perspective," in *Primacy in the Church: The Office of Primate and the Authority of Councils,* vol. 2, ed. John Chryssavgis (Yonkers, NY: St Vladimir's Seminary Press, 2016), 531–53.

[26]Thanks to its affirmation by the Holy Spirit, all the elements of the synod had also acquired the name "holy" (commemoration, horos, fathers, etc.), even though by nature they are not holy.

[27]The sole exception was St Augustine, whose lone case was due to his personal reputation. See *Acta Conciliorum Oecumenicorum* 1.1.8.

neglect the epistles of the five patriarchs, nor to violate the announced catalogue of themes.

4. As elucidated during the ecumenical councils and contrary to the Western theology of conciliarity that endorses "primacy" over "conciliarity," Orthodox theology—as developed by iconophiles and the other theologians—perceives the Truth that the councils express as the "relational" reality. A true council is one that does not seek automatic verification in any way, but seeks only a reception by the individual churches. Synodality-conciliarity involves participation and communion between the churches. When one council seeks its own truth, it loses its ecumenicity (for example, the Councils in 449 and 754), because in the long run, the future decides the past and determines our perception of the past. Any conciliarity that hinges upon its own legality, virtues, qualifications, proceedings, and so on is wrong and has nothing to do with the synodality of our Church. From these observations, it becomes obvious that the source par excellence of synodality-conciliarity is found in the Divine Eucharist.

5. In the imperial *sacra* of the Seventh Ecumenical Council (read at the first session), in one phrase, we see the connection between synodality and the Eucharist. The Eucharist hands down the testament of faith, while synodality safeguards it from deviations by offering a correct hermeneutical framework.

> On this account we have, by the good will and permission of God, caused you, his most holy Priests, to meet together—you who are accustomed to dispense his Testimony in the unbloody sacrifice [the Eucharist]—that your decision may be in accordance with the definitions of former Councils who decreed rightly, and that the splendor of the Spirit may illumine you in all things.[28]

[28]". . . Συνηγάγομεν ὑμᾶς τοὺς ὁσιωτάτους αὐτοῦ ἱερεῖς, τοὺς διατιθεμένους τὴν

This is how the double purpose of the ecumenical councils is inter-preted: panegyrical acceptance of those who correctly believe in Christ, something that is affirmed in the eucharistic unity, and the cutting off from the body of the Church of all those who deviate from the faith (and are thus sanctioned by eucharistic excommunication).

All Church councils—episcopal, local, and ecumenical—are nei-ther above nor against but always *in* the Church, dependent always on the *ecclesial reception* of the councils' decisions by the entire body. This simple idea captures the core insight of ecclesial synodality.

Conciliar Criterion of the Truth

We have said that there is no criterion of Truth other than a conciliar one. However, today few people care about or make that differentia-tion. This creates a real dilemma: who, in the end, expresses the *truth* of the Church and counters the individuals or groups who *pretend* to express the truth of the Church? In the Church, we do not have teach-ings, except for those which have been verified through a council. It's important to remember this as we go on to examine the role of author-ity in this situation.

From this observation springs a series of truths that are relevant to our subject:

1. A council is a solution to (or way out of) any problem of the Church. If we do not say this, we will omit the truth that is in the very hypostasis of our Church. Such has always been the life of the Church, and we cannot erase such a great truth. "Brother, maybe you are cor-rect, or maybe not, but the council will decide." But if the council is

διαθήκην αὐτοῦ ἐπί θυσίαις ἀναιμάκτοις . . ." (Mansi, *Sacrorum Conciliorum* 7:1003). *The Divine Sacra sent by the Emperor Constantine and Irene to the Most Holy and Most Blessed Hadrian, Pope of Old Rome*, in Labbe and Cossart Concilia, tom. VII., col. 49, Eng. trans. in *Nicene and Post-Nicene Fathers*, Second Series, vol. XIV, 530.

not in the right, another council is needed to do this. For example, the Council of Hieria (754) was "replaced" (corrected and rejected) by the Seventh Ecumenical Council (787). This was an essential moment that illumines the dilemma of who, ultimately, has the right to decide about the Truth. During the fifth century AD, discussions were taking place about Nestorianism. For years, Nestorius (patriarch of Constantinople from 428 to 431) accused St Cyril of Alexandria of being a heretic, while St Cyril wrote him letters, addressing him as "*my concelebrant.*"[29] And at the Council of Alexandria, St Cyril even called him "brother and concelebrant." If St Cyril had claimed that he possessed the Truth, he would not have waited for a council. It was only after the Council of Ephesus (431) that he ceased calling him "brother and concelebrant." Therefore, if a contemporary council disputes (or negates) an ecumenical council, a new ecumenical council should be called to evaulate that claim.

2. In the Orthodoxy of today, where the denial of institutions is widespread, it is often necessary to demonstrate the constitutional character of the Church expressed through the convening of a synod. The fathers of the Holy and Great Council in Crete figured this out, and the proposal they put forth is a logical yet profound extension of our discussion.[30] As opposed to St Cyprian of Carthage (third century), St Basil the Great (fourth century), and many others, who always scrutinized their beliefs through the councils, various "charismatics" of today pretend to already know what and where the truth is. There are multiple historical examples showing how great saints of the Church

[29]"To the most religious and beloved of God, fellow minister Nestorius, Cyril sends greeting in the Lord" (*Ep.* 2 [PG 77:43]).

[30]This council clearly pointed out, "[P]reserving the true Orthodox faith is provided only through the system of councils, which was always in the Church represented by a competent and final judge for questions regarding the faith. . . ." (based on Canon 6, Second Ecumenical Council).

relied on the councils (instead of relying on their own wishes) to verify the truths of the Church. For example:

a) The Church of Carthage faced schism due to the arbitrariness of some confessors who, relying on their own authority, challenged the authority of the episcopacy. They were misusing the tradition that originated in the Church of Carthage and was approved by the Councils in Numidia around AD 200 that confessors may receive into the Church those who have fallen away or been excommunicated by a bishop. St Cyprian did not approve of that practice, but he considered that the question should be solved by a council. Several confessors of the faith, taking advantage of St Cyprian's absence due to persecution, began issuing various letters of reconciliation (*libelli pacis*) to some of those who had fallen away during a time of oppression (and there were a considerable number of them). On the other hand, St Cyprian had advised these people not to approach Communion *until a council had been convened* but to accept, rather, the status of penitents in the Church.

b) St Basil the Great differentiated a *heresy* from a *schism*, which was contrary to the belief of the Council of Carthage (under St Cyprian), which called for the new baptism of heretics (*anabaptisma*). St Basil said that they should not be baptized, but he suggested that a "greater" (μεῖζον) synod be called (a council with a greater number of bishops) so that they could rightfully decide.

c) At the beginning of the fourth century, we note that *councils* received much greater significance, and St John Chrysostom is an indicative example.

The second and final exile of John Chrysostom (404) was based on the consideration that his return from his first exile (403) had not been annulled by a council. His enemies produced a canon to support their argument: canon 18 of the council of Antioch (341). John's followers were quick to point out that this was a canon emanating from an Arian council directed against the saintly Athanasius.[31]

Palladius' *Dialogue on the Life of St John Chrysostom* recounts how in a dispute before the Emperor Arcadius, one of John's followers challenged their enemies to say that they subscribed to the faith of the council (that had decreed this canon).[32]

d) The same "conciliar logic" urged Theodoret of Cyrus, who had been condemned at Ephesus (449), to prove his orthodoxy through a council. "He had written in praise of the Tome [of Leo]; he had brought his case to the notice of prominent officers of state, and urged them to persuade the new Emperor *to summon a General Council*, that the cause for which he stood might be vindicated."[33]

[31]Van Nuffelen, "The Rhetoric of Rules and the Rule of Consensus," in *Episcopal Elections*, 248.

[32]*Dial. de vita Chrysost.* 9 (SC 341:183–84). Cited in Van Nuffelen, ibid. Curiously, St Hilary of Poitiers (350–67), who was contemporary with the Antiochian Council, called this gathering *synodus sanctorum* (*De Synodis* 32 [PL 10:504]). There is a debate whether this Council was Arian or not (see D. D. Charles Joseph Hefele, *A History of the Councils of the Church: Volumes 1 to 5* [Edinburgh: T&T Clark, 1896]). Nevertheless, as Bishop Atanasije Jevtić holds (*The Holy Canons of the Church* [in Serbian] [Belgrade, 2005], 252), from a group of the bishops from this Council emerged those bishops from the East who fought the decisive fight against Arianism and its extreme wing, Anomianism, such as Sts Meletius of Antioch and the Cappadocians, as well as the members of the Council of Constantinople in 381. The canons of this council, with good reason, had entered the canonical collection of the Church.

[33]Sellers, *The Council of Chalcedon*, 124. So, when the case of Theodoret came before the Council, "the Bishop pleaded that he should be allowed to explain his faith, but there were those many in the assembly who, unable to forget that this was he who had dared to attack the blessed Cyril and had been the friend of Nestorius, again and again shouted him down, and demanded that he should pronounce forthwith a direct anathema on his former friend. This at last he did, and, Marcian having confirmed the Council's verdict, Theodoret was reinstated as Bishop of Cyrus" (Sellers, *The Council of Chalcedon*, 124; cf. Mansi, *Sacrorum Conciliorum*, 7:185ff.).

e) By the same token, Theophanes in his *Chronographia* describes how Emperor Leo convened a *silentium* in 730 against the holy and venerable icons and had invited the most holy Patriarch Germanus, thinking that he could persuade the patriarch to sign a condemnation of the icons. Instead of doing so, Germanus expounded correctly the true doctrine, resigned from the episcopacy, surrendered his *pallium*, and said: "If I am Jonah, cast me into the sea. For without an ecumenical council it is impossible for me, O emperor, to innovate in matters of faith."[34]

Similar examples can be found in many other councils, showing that each individual who goes against the councils can (and, perhaps, should) be asked, "Who are you, sir, that you are above the council? How will you prove that you are right?" In reality, it turns out that fear of conciliarity is one of the most common reasons for resistance to councils, and vice versa.

3. It is not an overstatement to say that none of the councils understood their task to be that of a systematic theologian, who "systematizes" faith (the Seventh Ecumenical Council is a good example). On the contrary, the function of the council as an institution in the Church was and remains as a *communio* (κοινωνία) in faith in the Eucharist. Subsequently, they transfer and inject the dogmas in every contemporary era—for dogmas have life. Every epoch and generation is called to live by the dogmas in its own manner, without introducing new dogmas. Ever since the first centuries in the Church, Orthodox bishops from the ends of the known world would come to the Holy and Great Councils as bearers of the *charisma* of the cosmic transfiguration of the world—not as "delegates" from a series of ethnic Churches but

---

[34] *The Chronicle of Theophanes Confessor*, trans. Cyril Mango and Roger Scott (Oxford: Clarendon Press, 1997), 565.

as hierarchs of the *conciliar-catholic* episcopacies, which are identified with the One, Holy, Catholic, and Apostolic Church.

4. It is for this same reason that the Church had bestowed ecumenical authority not only to the bishops, but also to some Holy Fathers. These days, many people say that one saint was sole bearer of Truth during a certain time period or crisis of the Church. For example, one of the participants in the debate in Crete recalled St Maximus the Confessor (580–662), who at one moment in history was, so to speak, the sole bearer of Truth in the Orthodox East. This sort of statement is a logical problem. Namely, even though it is true that St Maximus at that given time expressed the Church, we can say that it was so in actuality only because the Sixth Ecumenical Council occurred *a posteriori* to proclaim it.[35]

5. It is said that the council expresses the faith, but, as it turns out, the faith must also be expressed through the council. The God-bearing fathers and theologians were "instruments of the Spirit," not as an indication of their virtues, but because in the holy council they "delivered the mystery of theology plainly to the Church."[36] The affirmation of a father in a holy council is what justifies him having the title of "ecumenical teacher."

---

[35]"There is no question that Maximus regarded the institutional structures of the Church as important: his involvement with Pope Martin in calling the Lateran Synod in 649 is evidence for this. . . . He may well have thought that, in the end, the truth would find synodical support and may well have thought that Rome and its pope would play a central role in this final victory for the true faith, but in his lifetime this could only be a matter of hope and prayer—which should not be underestimated" (Andrew Louth, "The Views of St Maximus the Confessor on the Institutional Church," in *Knowing the Purpose of Creation through the Resurrection: Proceedings of the Symposium on St Maximus the Confessor*, 354, 355).

[36]*Doxastikon of the Praises*, Orthros, Sunday of the Holy Fathers, *Pentecostarion*, ed. Holy Transfiguration Monastery, 369.

Though people of today seem to doubt the need for and question the validity of councils, the Orthodox (before undergoing the corruption of secularism) had no difficulty whatsoever with reverencing the Holy and Great Councils. St Athanasius the Great is an eloquent example of this. For forty years (330–370), he labored ascetically both in the East and in the West with all his might in order to protect the "*homoousion*," but it was at the Council of 362 in Alexandria that he finally approved the formula of the "Easterners" of "three *hypostases* in one *physis*." St Athanasius the Great spoke the truth, but had the First or Second Ecumenical Council not justified his position, how would we have known that he was speaking the truth? The great significance of this Council of St Athanasius in 362 (this hierarch—let us remember!—had stressed two decades before the Second Ecumenical Council the need for an *amendment* to the Nicene Creed) lies in the fact that two opposing groups were brought to acceptance and confession not simply of the Nicaean faith, but to a *new interpretation of this faith*.[37] Thanks to this, we have "Neo-Nicenes" (for instance, the great Cappadocian Fathers), as well as the "neo-Chalcedonians," and in the twentieth century the "Neopatristic" theologians (Georges Florovsky, St Justin Popović, John Meyendorff—just to name a few). This conciliar methodology of healing a schism clearly applies the principle of *re-reception* or *new-reception* of the faith of the Fathers.

This leads us to a simple but astounding point: Someone must confirm that something *is*. Without a council we cannot be certain about anything, and without a council the Church would be disassembled. Would any of the abovementioned fathers have been a saint if they had been accepted as teachers by individual groups, but had not received confirmation from the holy councils? The answer is most

---

[37]See Atanasije Jevtić, "St Athanasius the Great and the Council in Alexandria in 362," *Na putevima Otaca I* [in Serbian], 63–152.

likely no. The rulings issued by universal councils become binding on all Christians.

Concluding Remarks

We have discussed here some of the most fundamental questions that we heard in the recent comments about the Holy and Great Council in Crete. There is an overabundance of false information regarding some important aspects of the Great Council, such as the *composition* of the council, the *number* of its participants, the way of *signing*, the significance of episcopal *signatures*, the issue of *voting*, and more. Even now, some with unquestionable certainty express *a priori* judgments on these issues without consulting historical data, which would in fact contradict them. These contentions, too, require comment, because they raise broad questions and are connected with misunderstandings that have a wider circulation.

There is, for example, a divergence of opinion between the position of Metropolitan Hierotheos of Nafpaktos,[38] on the one hand, and other scholars such as Metropolitan Maximos Vgenopoulos and especially Metropolitan Chrysostomos of Messinia,[39] on the other, as to the role

[38]I believe that my article addresses some of the concerns of M. Vlachos (in his article "The Decisions of the Hierarchy of the Church of Greece on the 'Holy and Great Council' and Their Fate. "As for the new ecclesiology explicated by Crete, it is nothing less than a new, insidious Papalism. First of all, it solidifies the idea that one bishop (in this case the Patriarch of Constantinople) can call a Council." This is wrong, because it was the agreement of all Orthodox Churches to convene the council; this one bishop could not cancel the council when some Churches asked for it, for he was obliged by the agreement of all Orthodox Churches. For Vlachos's second ("no one bishop had a vote at all; all he had at best was a chance to voice a concern about his particular church's final vote") and third points ("because the entire college of bishops were not invited then it implies that they are not equal and hence not real bishops"), see my answers below.

[39]Metropolitan of Messenia, Chrysostomos Savvatos, *The Holy and Great Council*

played by the *episcopacy* in the councils. It appears that the subject of a "bishop-council" remains a controversial one, particularly with regard to the Holy and Great Council.

Through the exploration of historical councils, my ultimate aim here was to set out the basic perspective of conciliarity, which, in summary, includes the following:

a) The number of participants was never decisive for the significance or reception of an ecumenical council, and it is *incorrect to say that all bishops were invited to those councils.* This is obvious from the discrepancies between presence and signatory lists (the lists of those bishops and their representatives who signed their approval of the council's Definition of Faith).[40]

b) The principle of *one bishop–one vote* (εἷς ἀνὴρ–μία ψῆφος)[41] was not absolute (the Acts of the Councils are clear in this respect, and the role of *acclamation*[42] and common vote, κοινὴ ψήφος, must be taken into consideration). Actually, both at Chalcedon and in Crete, the acts of the meetings were composed of both the sermons or the addresses and acclamations, both being essential to the conclusions. This helps to explain the fidelity of Crete to the ecumenical councils.

---

of the Orthodox Church as an Expression of the Synodal Self-Conscience of the Orthodox Church [in Greek] (Athens, 2017).

[40]Cf. Anna Crabbe, "The Invitation List to the Council of Ephesus and Metropolitan Hierarchy in the Fifth Century," *Journal of Theological Studies* 32 (1981): 369–400.

[41]Cf. the structure εἷς ἀνὴρ–μία ψήφος established by some modern thinkers. This implies the *modern* subject-object split and locates the question of Truth in the bridge between conciliar universality and individual topicality (bishop as deciding on behalf of his diocese).

[42]At Chalcedon, the Creeds of Nicaea and Constantinople and Cyril's letters to Nestorius (*Obloquuntur*) and John of Antioch (*Laetentur coeli*) were received with acclamation. Leo's Tome was also greeted with shouts of approval. On the other hand, no attention was paid to the Illyrians, who pleaded that mercy should be shown to the heads of the Synod of Ephesus, and even to Dioscorus. Cf. Sellers, *The Council of Chalcedon*, 111.

c) The *signatures* had more of a *symbolic value* (which is still not insignificant) than an essential role (for example, in the Acts of the Councils we see that some bishops' signatures are on some sessions while on others they are absent, and nobody mentions this as a problem).

d) *Voting* at the historical councils was principally determined by the vote or stance of the head (primate or senior bishop) of the delegation of the local churches. Wider geographical regions, such as a patriarchate or archdiocese, would sometimes express themselves with one vote per region and in that way they expressed their *consensus*, or *phronēma*; a good example of this is the Patriarchate of Alexandria at Chalcedon.[43] Ancient synods were meant to be consensual. The primary purpose of the holy canons was to remove obstacles to the emergence of a true consensus, and not the creation of a full-fledged procedure.[44] This does not, however, imply that procedure played no role at all.

e) Particular bishops *not signing* a conciliar decision, or opposing it (remember the Roman legates at Chalcedon), did not affect the final outcome of a council or its reception. Each bishop was allowed or invited to offer his *sententia*, his official response. A final vote was usually not necessary, for the *sententiae* were most often issued in unanimity, the result of previous negotiation.[45]

---

[43]Ancient Epitome of Canon 30 of Chalcedon has the following: "It is the custom of the Egyptians that *none subscribe without the permission of their Archbishop.* Wherefore they are not to be blamed who did not subscribe the Epistle of the holy Leo until an Archbishop had been appointed for them" (cf. Percival, *The Seven Ecumenical Councils*, 291).

[44]Cf. Van Nuffelen, "The Rhetoric of Rules and the Rule of Consensus," in *Episcopal Elections*, 257.

[45]"Like the Senate the council was a deliberative assembly, each bishop having equal rights in its discussions. Like the imperial magistrate who presided over the Senate, the principal bishop first read out a program designed to keep discussion to the point at issue. . . . The unanimous decision was circulated among the faithful in a

* * *

The Holy and Great Synod is a *communio ecclesiarum*, "the communion of churches," par excellence; it is the zenith of conciliarity, not only because it offers the churches the most visible and tangible union—eucharistic and doctrinal unity in Christ and the Holy Spirit—but also because it constitutes the portrayal of Pentecost. That is what the teaching of the fathers aspired to, which is the conciliar verification of their theology. This point is forgotten and overlooked by many contemporary theologians, even the Orthodox, who especially in our day tend to relate synodality to ideological declarations.

A council, as a feast, a criterion, and an event of the Church, is an opportunity for all to refresh and update the charismatic and dogmatic experience of the Church. In modern culture, where the existential question of man and society is posed in a strident way, the contribution of the Orthodox Church, which claims to be "the Church of the councils" (Florovsky, Karmiris, Schmemann) can be great. A Church that acts in a synodal way has to do with man, and not with an ideological movement. The new conciliar era enables us to take concrete steps to increase the voice of the local churches in the witness and governance of the universal Church.

Under such ecclesial conscience, the bishops of the Council in Crete displayed a self-conscious awareness (*phronēma*) of maintaining direct continuity with the work of previous councils (which they also cited in their Message, Encyclical, and other documents). Let us hope that the entire Orthodox world will grasp that the council is not a conference of administrative directors or experts, but a gathering of bishops: those who have an empirical function of spiritual paternity.

synodal letter. Bishops then felt themselves bound to abide by the decisions thus promulgated" (L. D. Davis, *The First Seven Ecumenical Councils [325–787]: Their History and Theology* [Collegeville, MN: Liturgical Press, 1983], 23).

PART IV

Art, Icon, and Paradox

Is There Truth in Art?

> Every work of art comes into being in the same
> way as the cosmos. . . . The creation of the work
> of art is the creation of the world.
> —Wassily Kandinsky

A FRENCH PHOTOGRAPHER takes a picture of a young lady pianist, right after a shell has pierced the wall of her room. An Orthodox iconographer takes the image and creates a painting of it. Now, the girl is depicted bending forward, in the moment of creativity, composing a new melody; while her eye reads the music, with undivided attention to the sound of her elastic and cyclically shaped piano, the candle is being extinguished by the explosion. Despite the black color of nothingness below the piano—reminiscent of the horrors of the war—everything conveys the desire for creativity through the ecstatic expression of pianist.[1] When we stand full of admiration before a work of art, we often ask ourselves how it is possible for a single person to create such a stupendous piece of art.

It is true that the origin of both divine and human creativity occurs in a space we cannot access. Yet, although we are unable to explain this secret of fashioning, artists can still try to relive the moment of creation. As we run, like the rest of the world today, along the digital pathways of computer screens and a confusing network of images, it

[1] Fr Stamatis Skliris, "A Lady Pianist," 2016, acrylic on canvas, Athens, 2016, http://holyicon.org/images/01/paintings-recent-works/029.jpg, accessed on June 20, 2017.

may be time to stop, to wait by the side of that busy path for a while. It is time to look at creation with a freedom that does not distort the identity of the beings.

Along those lines, three modern Orthodox icon theorists—Fr Stamatis Skliris, George Kordis, and Fr Maximos Constas[2]—have an irresistibly fascinating story to tell. If we let ourselves into their relentlessly personal approach to the Truth with humble obedience, then the mystery of two natures united in one hypostasis will be revealed to us. Let's walk with them down the concealed footpath that leads to mystical places, beyond the sanctuary veil and the well of the Annunciation, among the gold-lit corners of Hagia Sophia, and then ascend Sinai's stairways to the doorstep of the Pantocrator. There we will realize how the interdependence of the verbal and the visual in Byzantine civilization is an antipode to the confusing digital pathways and networks of contemporary virtual reality. What unifies the theoretical approach of Skliris, Kordis, and Constas is a lucid treatment of diverse topics, including questions about the enigmatic face of Christ in a sixth-century icon, the art of Chalcedon and the Seventh Ecumenical Council, aesthetic and ontological light, and more. All of their works are centered around the notion of *paradox, revelation,* and *surprise* in a compelling diapason of themes.

Paradox, Revelation, and Surprise

There is something very unusual about the icon and its theology. Icons have recently grown in popularity, which is inevitable given that even

[2]Stamatis Skliris, *In the Mirror: A Collection of Iconographic Essays and Illustrations* (Los Angeles: Sebastian Press, 2007); George Kordis, *Icon as Communion* (Brookline, MA: Holy Cross Orthodox Press, 2011); Maximos Nicholas Constas, *The Art of Seeing: Paradox and Perception in Orthodox Iconography* (Los Angeles: Sebastian Press, 2014).

human thought is essentially *iconic*. One is reminded of Patriarch Nicephorus (from the eighth century), who believed that "not only Christ, but the whole universe disappears if neither circumscribability nor image exist."[3] When the Gospel began to spread among the ancient Greeks, it reversed their world view by answering their philosophical questions and offering an iconic ontology. Constas argues persuasively that every aspect of existence is *iconic* and that the *paradox* of the Incarnation was addressed and resolved only in visual-iconic terms. "In using images to overthrow the power of images, the icon seeks to disrupt habituated ways of seeing, to subvert the hegemony of naturalistic representation, and so summon the eye to a new mode of vision."[4] Humans are created in the image of God, but God also presents himself as truth in an iconic way ("conformed to the likeness of his Son," from Rom 8.29). Why? Because human freedom refuses to see God (or the cosmos) as representing an objective *something*, and wants to see him as a dynamic *how*, as a mode of *free* revelation.

Einstein allegedly said, "What really interests me is whether God had any choice in the creation of the world."[5] Indeed, must the physical universe have necessarily existed as it is, or could it have been created in another way? Today almost all scientists believe that the universe could indeed have been otherwise, and no logical reason exists as to why it has to be as it is. It seems, therefore, that God creates not simply as a scientist, but as an *artist*,[6] which opens up a variety of

[3] "... μᾶλλον δὲ οὐδὲ Χριστός, ἀλλὰ τὸ πᾶν οἴχεται, εἰ μὴ περιγράφοιτο καὶ εἰκονίζοιτο," *Antirrheticus* 1.20 (PG 100:244D).

[4] Constas, *Seeing*, 22.

[5] Cf. *Fitness of the Cosmos for Life: Biochemistry and Fine-Tuning*, ed. John D. Barrow, Simon Conway Morris, et al. (Cambridge: Cambridge University Press, 2008), 97.

[6] Cf. Wassily Kandinsky: "Painting is like a thundering collision of different worlds that are destined in and through conflict to create that new world called the work. Technically, every work of art comes into being in the same way as the cosmos—by

symbolisms for the creation. The Scripture speaks of God's artistry at work: creation has all the characteristics of art, mostly because of the elements of *freedom*, *relation*, and *indeterminacy*. In fact, a modern approach with regard to the sciences has led to a "scientific ecology" that bypasses the rock of scientific materialism and the whirlpool of theological spiritualism. For this debate, a recent book by Nobel laureate Eric R. Kandel, called *Reductionism in Art and Brain Science: Bridging the Two Cultures*,[7] is very instructive, with the basic thesis that these two realms are not inseparably divided.

An artistic view negates the coincidence of the concept with the object of perception. By the same token, from the very beginning, an ecclesial (eschatological) view of truth reveals the experience of personal presence, in which the world is something we *experience* and not something we think about. Stefan Zweig in his *The Secret of Artistic Creation* explains the conception of a work of art as an inner process, a divine phenomenon, a mystery. "The only thing we can do is to reconstruct this act once it has taken place and even then it is possible to do so only to a certain extent."[8] Here Zweig's credo hints at the image of Genesis, where the miracle of a *creatio ex nihilo* is narrated. Only sporadically are human beings able to share in this miracle, and that is what transpires in art. Zweig positions Genesis and the origin of creation among the acts he considers to be miracles and goes on to talk about an

means of catastrophes, which ultimately create out of the cacophony of the various instruments that symphony we call the music of the spheres. The creation of the work of art is the creation of the world" (Wassily Kandinsky, *Complete Writings on Art* [Boston, MA: Da Capo, 1994], 373).

[7] See Eric R. Kandel, *Reductionism in Art and Brain Science: Bridging the Two Cultures* (New York: Columbia University Press, 2016).

[8] See Stefan Zweig, "The Secret of Artistical Creation, Lecture, USA 1938," in *Das Geheimnis de künstlerischen Schaffens* (Frankfurt am Main: Fischer Tachenbuchverlag, 1981), 230. Cited in Christine Berthold, "Stefan Zweig and the Secret of Artistic Creation," *Analecta Huserliana* LX, 214.

unfathomable and irrational miracle, because artists create entities that defy change.[9] "If you put your very existence into it, your sensitivity and humanity, it makes a sound distinctly yours," says Steve Lopez, in the film, *The Soloist*.[10] However, most of the time, art contradicts the mind, and we cannot determine whether it reflects the truth or not.

Is This True?

Philosophically, truth has traditionally been identified with "factual reality" (*adaequatio rei et intellectus*): what I say—or see—is true because it corresponds with reality. But reality is subject to change and corruption; it perishes. Imagine somebody telling you, "You are dying now." You would say, "That's nonsense!" But, when an artist depicts you in a state of dying, he or she undoubtedly expresses an *existential* truth. Even in Plato, truth dwells not in reality, but in the ideal world. Obviously, the definition of art depends on what you suppose your existence is like, or what your—the "beholder's"—eyes expect to see. This is precisely the point that Maximos Constas asserts: "Only things that contradict the mind are real."[11] In idealistic art, such as that of the Renaissance, the idea of physical beauty in nature is an ideal. In that sense, "human desire is never pure; it is never entirely without risk for the one who is drawn to beauty."[12] And yet, nature is corruptible and transient and circumscribed by death. Such art revels in change, corruption, and in the fact that nothing remains the same over time.

Now, how can one determine if one work of art is true and another is not? How can we judge the truth of the icons? Is there a means to

[9]See Berthold, "Stefan Zweig and the Secret of Artistic Creation," 214.

[10]A 2009 British-American drama film directed by Joe Wright, starring Jamie Foxx as Nathaniel Ayers and Robert Downey Jr. as Steve Lopez.

[11]Constas, *Seeing*, 10.

[12]Ibid., 11.

overcome the didactic, decorative, religious, and emotional function of art and reach the revelatory, *apocalyptic* truth which surprises us by its struggle to express the principle (*logos*) and the mode (*tropos*) of things?

In contrast with *natural art*, which idealizes the natural world and, therefore, is bounded by time, the icon is the truth presented in a way that is not controlled by our senses or our mind; you cannot conceive it. We can apply this to almost the whole of art except when it comes from an asphyxiatingly subjective unconscious. (To be clear, a faulty construction of reality is not a criterion for aesthetic evaluation.) Genuine art conveys the truth that is not passed through the mind, but rather provokes a readiness to be face-to-face with your existence. It is an "openness to another form which is different from me, which actively approaches me from outside of myself, offers itself to me as a gift."[13] This implies that, on this matter, we do not have a philosophical but an *experiential* answer to the question of how we can judge between false and true philosophical statements. For instance, the reality of Christ brings something ultimate that cannot be judged simply philosophically, since it is the *relation* what constitutes it. How are we to explain this?

We judge truth in art (for instance, in portraiture) by asking the question, "Is this accurate?" But usually we employ the naturalistic approach. For example, if you have a photograph of Christ and an icon-painting of Christ, which one is more truthful? If you have a naturalistic approach, you would certainly say, "The photograph." But, if you believe that non-naturalistic art is more true, then you point to the unconventional and apocalyptic truth.[14] It will therefore be instructive to consider the fact that *there is truth in art that doess not simply cor-*

[13]Ibid., 17.

[14]Cf. the sixth-century icon of the Sinai Christ with polarized facial expressions.

respond with the mind or reality. A definition of truth must point to "*relationality*" or referentiality to a common ground of existence that we share (that is, truth in existential terms).

Light and Shadow

Indeed, "the icon seeks to disrupt habituated ways of seeing, to subvert the hegemony of naturalistic representation, and so summon the eye to a new mode of vision."[15] Skliris's *In the Mirror* is a powerful illustration of how one moves from the Byzantine icon—where the gaze is transcendent and ambiguous, and surpasses the feelings of this world—to his own icons, where the gaze comes out of the painted image and examines the observer,[16] without arresting the observer's vision.

Another aspect we must consider is the "photoconductive" interpretation of Byzantine aesthetics, that is, an interpretation based on the free and flexible conduction of light, which has wide-ranging implications for the problem of truth in the visual arts.

The reason for introducing photoconductivity here is not to delve into the intricacies of Byzantine art. Rather, the example of light, as we shall see, can provide a simple ground for extracting unexpected answers to the truth question. As Skliris notes, "Every revolutionary scientific discovery about the nature of light in modern times has been reflected in a corresponding revolutionary movement in Western art, as Western art is always concerned with the problem of natural lighting."[17]

[15]Constas, *Seeing*, 22. This requires, in Fr Maximos's words, "an engagement with the content of perception, an entry into the inner logic of what is seen or heard, a deepening into the interiority of the surface phenomenon" (*Seeing*, 17).

[16]Cf. Skliris, *Mirror*, 7, 68, 125, 129.

[17]Ibid., 169. "Not only does it offer a unitary explanation in that it interprets all the aesthetic and philosophical problems of Byzantine art on the basis of a single aesthetic axiom, that of light, but also, and more importantly, through light it establishes the

Light is among the most familiar yet least understood phenomena that humanity has ever encountered. We say that it warms; we say that it is knowledge; we try to shed it; we get desperate when we lose it. But what is light? To quote Terry Pratchett (in *Reaper Man*), "No matter how fast light travels, it finds the darkness has always got there first, and is waiting for it." Is this true? In some ways, it is. In other ways, it's not. Obviously, light is mostly responsible for making objects visually apparent. Yet, the definition of visual art depends not on light but on shadow. Shadow instills into art the constraints of all the natural laws at once: gravity, impenetrability, temporality, mutability, decay, and inertia. So, what we "know" thanks to shadow is the necessity—and not freedom—of structure. It is this magical spell of shadow that monopolizes the construction of a visual work of art.[18]

In a series of creative surprises, Byzantine art put an emphasis on the light, which always comes from a source outside the picture; "its incidence [is] always in parallel rays perpendicular to the picture plane and it always unite[s] what had hitherto been multiple planes into a single plane, in which all the action [is] depicted."[19]

Skliris's viewpoint is simple and compelling. The Byzantines do not "reverse" the perspective, as if there were an initial "normal" perspective of the Renaissance that Byzantine art somehow invalidates. On the contrary, with the revelation of the *increasing perspective*, we do not worry about the fragmentation of information given by the optical lens (which at each moment distinguishes only certain sides of an object). Natural artists in general (and Renaissance ones in particular) can deal only with the measurable properties of the space. Anything

connection between the graphic and chromatic elements of art, and between reason and sentiment" (ibid., 179).

[18]Cf. ibid., 179.

[19]Cf. ibid., 178.

else is simply not in the domain of physics. For the iconic knowledge, there is no front and sides and back.

After a bit of scholarly scurrying in response to this unusual observation, the defenders of Byzantine ontology settled down to their pragmatic approach, summarized well by Skliris. According to him, the first consequence of this photoconductivity in Byzantine art was that "the figures and all the other subjects of the picture (houses, trees, mountains, and so forth) never overlapped, never stood out [in] front [of] the rest, never overshadowed each other in accordance with the deterministic stratification imposed by the inexorable law of the rectilinear conduction of light: they were always placed *side by side*, at an equal distance from the viewer."[20] This explanation of Byzantine composition, arising through the inevitable disturbance instigated by the measurement process, has provided theologians with a useful intuitive guide as well as a powerful explanatory framework to be used in other specific facets (for example, in hagiography).

We can take this role that light plays in Byzantine icon-making and apply this logic in modern painting. Skliris handles it in a neoimpressionist manner, capturing Byzantine light with brushstrokes that emphasize dominant points in an impressionist manner. Although Skliris basically employs a dark Byzantine underpainting, adding to it light "accents" (illuminations), he still plays with colors in such an impressionist manner that his work gains a "non-determinism of color." He leaves sections of his painting uncolored and then makes these sections unpredictable and playful. Both Skiliris and Kordis overcome a

[20]Cf. ibid., 178. However, there remained "a kind of stratification based on size, in the sense that different elements of the composition were depicted on different scales: human figures bigger than the houses, trees and mountains round about, the principal saint bigger than the other figures, Christ bigger than the apostles. But this reflected only the artist's estimation of their relative importance to the subject of his picture" (ibid).

spirit that expresses itself in pure symmetry, or geometric patterns and arabesques. Instead, they propose a divine-human balance, avoiding any sort of "anthropolatry" in arts.[21]

Through this photoconductivity, ill-proportioned Byzantine icons ("earthen vessels")[22] have become the revealers of transcendent truths, signaling "the advent of a distinctive new aesthetic."[23] This ontological aesthetic is expanded to church architecture, the symbolism of liturgical movements and gestures, and other liturgical and theological manifestations. As such it could not be ignored by theologians and artists.

Icon as a Presence to Which One Can Relate

From understanding the icon as a transparent "window to eternity," we are led to its role as "mirror," where objects are seen in dynamic relation to their eschatological prototype. The icon is a hypostatic presence to which one can relate, which is at the same time *transcendent*. Having said that, the icon leads beyond the idol. "In concretizing the splendor of the visible, the idol dazzles and so arrests our vision, confining it within a closed, self-referential system, allowing us to see nothing outside itself."[24]

This encounter with the divine, in paradox and ambiguity, is a matter of *relation* rather than logical argumentation. Since our relation in history is also *iconic*, not direct (this perceived "weakness" of the icon is precisely its "strength"), we cannot have a logical proof for truth; instead there is *a decision one makes to relate*. Skliris, Kordis,

[21]Interestingly, an inscription in Greek on the fresco of the Church of Christ in Arbanasi (seventeenth c.) says, "The Holy Third Ecumenical Council of 200 Fathers took place in Ephesus under Theodosius against Nestorius the anthropolater (κατὰ Νεστορίου τοῦ ἀνθρωπολάτρου)."

[22]Cf. 2 Cor 4.7.

[23]Constas, *Seeing*, 15.

[24]Ibid., 21.

and Constas inventively interlace *apophatic* and *cataphatic*, text and image, meaning and perception, exegesis and poetics. Yet, for them, the apophatic without the cataphatic makes no sense: iconicity is apophatic because it cannot be grasped intellectually; it's cataphatic when approached experientially.[25] It is, indeed, a wondrous asymmetry expressed through art. This, however, requires "a certain degree of commitment, of patience, of time, a waiting on the object that is before us, a humble obedience to it, for there is a sense in which it offers itself to me only as much as I renounce my own ability to grasp and comprehend it."[26] Therefore, the iconic approach presupposes that one accept *a presence to which one can relate*. This was the argumentation of the theologians (among them, Sts Maximus the Confessor, John Damascene, and Theodore the Studite) throughout the history of Byzantium. This relation is bidirectional, Constas asserts: "It is no longer simply I who see, but also I who am seen. The 'object' of my vision has now become a subject, it approaches me from outside myself, and draws out its implications in me."[27]

Here we tackle interpretive challenges of the highest order. An icon or symbol is a presence hidden behind corruptible things; it reveals the *hypostatic presence* (i.e., the truly personal and not simply phenomenal, or natural), and the icon establishes this relationship (συμβάλλειν) with us. For this reason, each icon has a name; anonymous icons are not to be used or prayed with.[28] But the character of this presence is

[25]"Thus an understanding of Byzantine art presupposes the amorous admiration of existence which is implied in the Byzantine icon, yet this requires an Orthodox apophatic aesthetic, which of course cannot be described by Kantian or Hegelian aesthetic categories" (Skliris, *Mirror*, 40).

[26]Constas, *Seeing*, 17.

[27]Constas, *Seeing*, 32.

[28]Cf. "ἀφανισθέντος τοῦ ἐν αὐτῇ ὁρωμένου ὁμοιώματος, ἐφ' ᾧ ἡ προσκύνη σις, ἔμεινεν ἡ ὕλη ἀπροσκύνητος, ὡς μηδὲν κοινωνοῦσα τῷ ὁμοιώματι" (Theodore the Studite, *Letter to Plato* 7 [PG 99:504D]).

that the person maintains its transcendence so that its hypostasis is not exhausted in the material nature of the icon. If we understand icons as a simple means of *reminding* (psychologically or mentally) us of persons and events (as is the case in Roman Catholic art)—so that only the thought of a person who prays is turned to them—then we deprive the material world of God's presence in Christ. The Church reflects, iconizes the mystery of the Holy Trinity. The great fathers of the Church link the Church with the Trinity, having as a link the Hypostasis of the Son and Word of God—Christ, a "defenseless man who 'had no beauty' (Is 53:2) and who for that reason is the 'Icon of the Invisible God' (Col 1:15)."[29]

So the iconicity (symbols, types, the making of icons, etc.) is more true to theology than any sort of "immaterial" approach (noetic prayer, logical argumentation, etc.) inherent in various forms of spiritualism, since that approach always requires the material visualization that no ecclesial symbolism can exist without. The Uncreated does not communicate directly with the created but through various forms of symbols that are created and hypostasized in the person of the Son. The Areopagite notes, "It is impossible for the divine ray to otherwise illumine us except by being anagogically concealed in a variety of sacred veils."[30] Only in the *eschaton* we will see God—but who dares to say "*only him*"?—as he truly is, because, as St Maximus the Confessor says, the truth is eschatological.

---

[29]Constas, *Seeing*, 12.

[30]Ibid., 32 [quoting *Celestial Hierarchy* 1.2 (PG 3:121B)—*Ed.*]. See also Fr Maximos's interpretation of the notion "symbol," based on St Maximus the Confessor and St Gregory Palamas ("St Maximus the Confessor: The Reception of His Thought in East and West," in *Knowing the Purpose of Creation through the Resurrection*, 51).

The Future of Iconic Ontology

If one accepts the Resurrection, one arrives at a vision of reality that is without death. In order to do that, one must *purify* the mind and senses of any illusions of reality, according to Constas, in "an act of self-denial, of continuous self-surrender, which at the same time is a progressive entrance into the mystery of that which makes itself present to me."[31] As Philippians makes clear, the act of radical self-emptying anticipates, and in a sense already is, the triumph over death.[32] An icon bridges the chasm between Creator and creation only through the intervention of the person of Christ, in whom there is the paradoxical coexistence of mercy and judgment. Since icons depict not natures per se but persons, Christian symbolism differs from pagan symbolism because the latter believes that the *nature* bridges the chasm on its own.

Many of the same formal characteristics that brand modern art exist also in the Byzantine icon. It is true that "the radical revision of the classical aesthetic canon was part of a much more comprehensive picture, of which the icon is an evocative symbol."[33] At the same time, the Orthodox Tradition anticipated all the elements that characterized modern and postmodern art.[34] It spoke the visual language of modernity and contained it in a *unifying* way, not analytically and fragmentarily (as it is in modern art). The icon was initially a surrealist painting. It possessed a strong differentiation of warm and cold colors (that is, complementarity), colored and dark shadows, and strong rays of light in the form of parallel white-lighting accents at prominent points. Even small, distinct dots of pure color, known as pointillism,

[31]Constas, *Seeing*, 17.
[32]Phil 2.9–10.
[33]Constas, *Seeing*, 22.
[34]An overview of these anticipations can be found in Stamatis Skliris, *U ogledalu i zagonetki* [in Serbian] (Belgrade, 2005), 493–507.

were not unknown to Byzantium. Byzantine painting knew the mechanism by which the disciple of El Greco, Cezanne, introduced the *cubist* interpretation of art space, which led to Picasso's cubism, but Byzantine painting used this mechanism without dissolving the unity of the existent into its geometrical elements. Byzantine art was non-naturalistic or even abstract (abstracting the elements of corruption) from its inception. It also knew expressionism from the very beginning (for instance, the big eyes even in catacombs, taken from the mask of theater; or the portrait of Christ of Sinai in which the "psychologization" of the divine-human drama is avoided, so that the riddle of human destiny finds a dignified solution). There are big eyes, emphatic long noses, strong expressions, and, very often, elements of hyperbole, but the whole approach eschews the psychological for the heuristic.

Iconic ontology is largely absent in today's discourse about icons. Constas is right when he maintains that "it is only by recovering the true iconicity of creation that we can hope to find healing for our damaged sensibility."[35] We can say the same regarding ecclesiology: by retrieving iconicity in the Church, we can reestablish the link between the Church and the Kingdom of God. This shift in perspective enables us to rediscover the true meaning of *iconicity*; it points to a plethora of expressive, symbolic, and pedagogical possibilities for ecclesial art (liturgical symbolism, icon-making, church architecture, etc.).

Theologians have long neglected art as a way of expressing theology. We *should* use art as a means of theologizing, our guides strongly suggest. They think it is not only more faithful to the Orthodox tradition, but also to the Western tradition.

A careful consideration of iconography by Stamatis Skliris and George Kordis and of the art studies of Maximos Constas helps us to adequately assume the complex aesthetics of Byzantine iconography

[35]Constas, *Seeing*, 29.

and to open up pathways into a new ecclesial synthesis of ontology, semiotics, phenomenology, and aesthetics.[36] God in art carries "the emphatic assurance of his real presence among us."[37] As a veritable treasure, the contributions of these three figures can have far-reaching effects on every level of ecclesial life and may even reach broader, cross-cultural contexts.

Art is meant to challenge the reality we create and to uncover an existential reality common to all: "the work of art remains a concrete, unified, spiritual vision of the experience of life."[38] Great art is not appreciated immediately, because it reveals something true. It is only in the future that its truth is confirmed and proved. The same is valid for many other things: Christopher Columbus traveled without knowing where he was heading and returned home without knowing where he had been. Only the "future" confirmed the truth about his voyage.

---

[36]Skliris ascends from the very beginnings of iconography (catacombs, Dura Europos, Sinai, etc.) and from classical Hellenic presumptions of iconography, striving to revitalize the initial solutions and choices made by early Christian art. Rather than following the ready-made mannerisms that were formed throughout the centuries, he chooses to observe the very first choices (examples: Skliris, *Mirror*, 30, 89, 91, 126, 210).

[37]Constas, *Seeing*, 106.

[38]Ibid., 31.

On Digital Iconicity

I can't believe I'm having this conversation with my computer.
—Theodore, *Her,* directed by Spike Jonze

I N A SCIENCE-FICTION film about computer dating, directed by Spike Jonze,[1] the character Theodore develops what will end up being a tragic relationship with Samantha, an intelligent computer operating system personified through a female voice. The mirroring formation of the ego is known to have existed since the depths of prehistory.[2] Yet now, as portrayed in the film *Her,* the love of a human for a fictitious being is enabled by modern technology, which stages reality in such a way that existential emptiness is artificially substantialized in a more dramatic way.

The phenomenon of the image or icon has recently grown in popularity, which is inevitable given that everything, our thoughts included, is essentially *iconic*. In a society obsessed with multimedia illusions, where visual pollution of every kind has obscured our real capacity to see, it is difficult to witness a true icon. The same pollution keeps our daily lives enslaved to the natural world as opposed to an iconic ethos (of which the icon is an evocative symbol) bequeathed from the Orthodox Tradition; this ethos, when lived as our Tradition intended,

---

[1] *Her,* directed by Spike Jonze (Burbank, CA: Warner Bros. Pictures, 2014), film.
[2] See more in Fr Vasileios Thermos, *Psychology in the Service of the Church: Theology and Psychology in Cooperation* (Los Angeles: Sebastian Press, 2017), 23.

leads to the affirmation of the other, and to humility before the other, whom we are invited to "honor above ourselves."[3]

How do we escape the main trap of the third millennium, which is nothing less than a total submission to the novel demands of modern technological man, without running the risk of living a para-eucharistic life? The increasing attempts to facilitate life through technological means in a digital culture (which can allow technology to enter our lives and control them) can eventually lead to a loss of both iconicity and the uniqueness of the person. This is a serious risk. In an era of transhuman technology (which includes artificial intelligence, cybernetics, mind uploading, and other technologies), each of us is on the path to becoming a tribe with one member. The glamorization of our lives via modern social media is just one of the symptoms of this self-idolatry.[4] The first iconoclastic controversy began within the Church, but social media may be thrusting upon us a new or resurgent iconoclasm that is overwhelming our experience with images that promote meaningless self-idolatry rather than viewing ourselves as icons of God. Remember, the iconoclast controversy was also about the rejection of true images/icons.

Technology is so omnipresent in contemporary life that we must consider whether it has become the very reality of life itself. It is difficult and arduous to decide how best to consider it both authentically and critically. The question that arises concerns a crucial theological and anthropological problem: *can humanity change the way it communicates without altering its own nature at some level?* Thanks to God-given freedom, man faces possibilities too difficult to handle, which are

[3]Rom 12.10.

[4]Cf. Michelangelo's words: "My fond imagination made art an idol and a tyrant to me" (see Gilles Neret, Μιχαὴλ Ἄγγελος, Taschen/Γνώση [Athens, 2004], 83). St Andrew of Crete wrote in the seventh century, "I have become an idol to myself" (*Canon of St Andrew of Crete*, Ode IV).

both paradoxical and multiple, since they simultaneously combine the prospects of good and evil. Yet, until recently, there was no discussion of the dangerous prospect of modifying nature and altering the human being. Yuval Noah Harari was able to work this out, and the answer he came to was enormously surprising.[5] Brain-computer interfaces and industrial robots threaten to change what it means to be human.

> No need to panic, though. At least not immediately. Upgrading Sapiens will be a gradual historical process rather than a Hollywood apocalypse. *Homo sapiens* is not going to be exterminated by a robot revolt. Rather, *Homo sapiens* is likely to upgrade itself step by step, merging with robots and computers in the process, until our descendants will look back and realise that they are no longer the kind of animal that wrote the Bible, built the Great Wall of China and laughed at Charlie Chaplin's antics. This will not happen in a day, or a year. Indeed, it is already happening right now, through innumerable mundane actions. Every day millions of people decide to grant their smartphone a bit more control over their lives or try a new and more effective antidepressant drug. In pursuit of health, happiness and power, humans will gradually change first one of their features and then another, and another, until they will no longer be human.[6]

Harari reports the alarming news that the issue is no longer whether we will have a good or bad human being, but whether we will have a human being whatsoever.

Keeping theology and communication in a synchronous dialogue and altering the models of communication in the Church can be posi-

---

[5]See Yuval Noah Harari, *Homo Deus: A Brief History of Tomorrow* (New York: HarperCollins, 2017).

[6]*Homo Deus*, 49.

tive if it is accomplished with theological awareness, sensitivity, and with the appropriate *criteria*. Without these, however, the transmission of the message of the Gospel to the world (the so-called "enculturation") can be a very hazardous endeavor. As classical ethics used to argue about, nothing is bad as such, and whether or not it is good depends on how the thing is used. But can this be applied to Internet technology? Can the Internet be good (not only useful) if we use it in a good way?

It appears that few, if any, even pose such a question, since it is fashionable to adopt new patterns without any deeper questioning or critical examination of them. Among ancient authors, the term *technology* (τεχνολογία) referred to oral and written communication. However, such kinds of communication after Gutenberg still did not lead to man's *alienation*—the medium remained constant, with only its proliferation increasing dramatically. Alienation emerged with a dramatic change in the use of technology by modern man. (Heidegger raised the question of technology in a compelling way.)[7] Only as man has infiltrated the realm of advanced technology—the huge industrialization of production and distribution, the challenge of nuclear energy, the omnipresence of computing, and so on—have we encountered the first (if we do not count the original fall of Adam and Eve) serious alienation of humankind. The Internet is the climax of this process, as man is alienated in a critical, if not existential, manner. Alienation is also reflected by the fact that modern man must enter into a system of "communication" and cannot "self-act" as before—he must follow a newly established communications protocol by submitting to digitalization (as opposed, for example, to freehand writing on a paper, which later can be wetted by a tear dropped on it). Furthermore, when

[7]M. Heidegger, *The Question Concerning Technology and Other Essays*, trans. W. Lovitt (New York and London: Garland, 1977).

everything is *inscribed* "online"—and when states and their authorities use electronic information in order to interfere in the private lives of citizens for the "sake of the common good"—what will happen to man's privacy and the protection of personal life?

Certainly, privacy is commonly understood as the ability to set boundaries around oneself, thereby affirming the self in an individualistic way. The right not to be exposed to unauthorized incursion of privacy (the collection of personal information for one's own purposes) by individuals, governments, or corporations is the foundation of *individual* freedom. *Personal* rights and freedoms, on the other hand, are more related to a nexus of relationships that respect and even affirm and confirm a human's very otherness. In that sense, the rights of the person are the most sacred rights of our civilization. When it comes to technology, it seems that both individual and personal rights are threatened. By emphasizing the reverence of human persons as icons of God, the Church, however, provides our culture with a prerequisite for its very survival.

Some have suggested that this alienation of man is demonic, in that each one of us, by taking part in the global system of the Internet, willingly becomes a *slave* of certain superpowers who might be able to form a world government, new world order, or other nefarious societal upheaval (which sounds apocalyptic, doesn't it?). Our evolution is strange. From the Platonic escape from ephemeral being, digital memory now leads to the extension of the mechanism of "panoptic control" into the past. Now, the Internet remembers what we prefer to be forgotten. Worse, the Internet may be selective in its memory.

As with any other revolution, the information revolution also devours its children. Freedom, enjoyed by man until recently, begins to be lost when the person is subordinated to the demands of technology, which, having caught us in its nets, reduces us to numbers on the omnipresent displays, while simultaneously enabling indiscriminate mechanisms for falsifying the truth that are unchecked. Some believe the blame is not to be placed on Facebook or Twitter or other social media platforms, because it is not a clever justification for a defeatist to place blame on technology as an undefined, impersonal spirit of history that imposes upon us certain behaviors. What is needed, instead, is a *willing* effort to control ourselves, because in the end *we* decide how to use our machines, and not vice versa. In the new culture of short (or distracted) attention and simulated, virtual relations, even time, which by definition should be "free," is filled with obligations to our "connectedness," and thus it ceases to be free.

In a new world of instant and "absolute" communication unbound from time and space, we suffer not only from unprecedented alienation but also from the desecration of time. What has happened to the sacredness of "now"? We ourselves have expelled it in various ways. Let us ask ourselves: when people obsessively photograph what is happening to them now, aren't they *postponing* their encounter with reality for later consumption? We can argue about this, but it's worth asking if the storing of digital material (photographs, music, movies, and TV series) emphasizes mere possession, which, in some cases, will become a *surrogate* for a real experience.

Certainly, every technological novelty brings both a promise and a risk. The many possibilities and benefits of this universal trend that enables the happiness of the individual can explain the ease with which people totally surrender themselves to the power of the media ecosystem. Is there anybody who can sober and encourage us to reexamine our newly obtained habits so that we become aware of the seriousness of the problem of cosmogenic changes in our cultural universe? Will anybody show us, even discreetly, how to avoid becoming mere numbers in this technological advancement and losing our uniqueness and unrepeatability? New technology, according to Neil Postman, always gives us something important, but it also takes away something that is important.[8]

In the ongoing debate over online euphoria on the American scene, one author warns, "As our cyber personalities grow more detailed, we see less of one another in person."[9] This debate sometimes leads to Hamlet's dilemma: *to be* in a virtual world, supported by cyber-worshipers, or *not to be*, as proposed by cyber-skeptics. It is easy not only to lean toward the opinion of those that zealously warn against technology's dangers, but also of those who with the same devotion defend technology, or even celebrate it. There is a "religiosity" in some people's conception of the text, cell phone, or email. However, instead of escaping from the digital culture, faced with Hamlet's dilemma, one might consider a counterproposal: *when* (or, better, *before*) we notice that, despite the convenience it offers, technology begins to deprive us of personal uniqueness by reducing us to numbers, *then* it is the moment to resist.

One approach to facing these challenges is the icon. If the icons of the Church comfort us with a divine tranquility, it is because they reveal deeper truth. Thanks to iconography, reality becomes "true" to the extent that it reflects the future, the eschatological state. But what place do icons occupy in the twenty-first century? Icons are no longer exclusive to Orthodox believers and their places of worship, since they have gained celebrity among Catholics and even Protestants. One might consider it a great success to see the world's largest museums offering their space for icon exhibitions and displaying them to a wide,

---

[8]See Neil Postman, *Amusing Ourselves to Death* (New York: Penguin, 1985).

[9]Lisa Lewis, "How E-Readers Destroyed My Love Life," *New York Times*, July 4, 2011, https://cityroom.blogs.nytimes.com/2011/07/04/complaint-box-how-e-readers-destroyed-my-love-life/, accessed September 26, 2015.

non-religious audience. However, in their display, meaning and reflection are blunted by the shallow celebration of an image, much like the fleetingness of Snapchat.

By cultivating icons, Christians celebrate a vision of life that is transfigured and changed in the Person of Jesus Christ. Every genuine work of art—and an icon is an obvious example—begins from *nothingness*[10] and *mask* and then attains to *being* and *person*. Apart from the extensive theological use of the term "person," this notion is very significant in dialogue with contemporary art and science. Only with the help of the term "person" can we demonstrate the dignity, uniqueness, and unrepeatability of man.[11] With its eschatological criterion, the icon corresponds with the genuine request of art: that the reality of things be represented visually not as they have been, or as they are, but as they might be. Byzantine iconography conveys exactly this vision of life to the society and culture in which we live: it expresses the spirit of a Christianized Hellenism that depicts persons as they *will be*, overcoming thus *protological* ontology (i.e., an ontology of death).

The great challenge that iconic ontology conveys to our "photographic logic" is that it requires us to consider a presence without death, something entirely unthinkable in our collective experience. The icon

---

[10]"I transformed myself in the zero of form and emerged from nothing to creation." (K. Malevich, "Kazimir Malevich: Suprematism," Guggenheim, retrieved October 15, 2016).

[11]"What did these names [of the Saints] mean? To that, I can now answer—that the person is everything. From the eternal perspective, all that is around and next to and on the person is neither numbered nor counted. The kingdoms and the states, treasures and crowns, embellishments and cultures, honors and glories: all of this is subordinated to the person, in the service of the person, worthless in comparison to the person. The saintly person is the soul of Christ's character, repeated, more or less, in many, many persons. The saints are cleansed mirrors in which the beauty and might of the majestic person of Christ is seen" (Saint Nikolai of Ohrid and Zhicha, *The Prologue of Ohrid* [Los Angeles: Sebastian Press, 2017], 5).

does not postpone but rather anticipates the future by relating it personally and ontologically. Icons are precious treasures in the Tradition, which testify to the *personal* relationship with God, and the viewpoint that a Christian doesn't belong solely to himself or herself, to his or her job, or to the ambitions of this world, but to God. Icons reveal that we are not alone or isolated, but that we belong to the communion of the saints, whom the Lord loves with such a great capacity that this world, with all of its temptations, cannot take away. This is truly the basis and goal of Christian prayer and compassion as philanthropic activity. Through these efforts one is led to the essential understanding of the relationship that each of us have with God, the world, and one another, as citizens of his Kingdom that is to come.

But, you might ask, what of it? The identification of the self-sameness of Christ with his image leads to the assertion that Orthodoxy is the Church and not an ideology. It is a gathering of the people and, particularly, a *eucharistic gathering of living icons*. This must be emphasized today: this icon is not an Internet (or online), virtual, and ephemeral illusion of communication, but the visible and true communication of the Kingdom. Such must be the future of Orthodoxy because such is the future Christ promises his Church. In the Eucharist, we are taught not only to venerate and greet the icons, but also the other members of the synaxis, not passing the living icons—people—by, but greeting and embracing them. So, the icon is indeed the proper method of viewing the world. Only this iconic approach will save Orthodoxy from becoming a secular organization, conforming to the image of the world and the docetism[12] of virtual communication.

---

[12]Docetism (from the Greek δοκεῖν/δόκησις, *dokein* [to seem], *dokēsis* [apparition, phantom]) is defined as the doctrine according to which the person of Christ, his historical and bodily existence, and thus above all the human form of Jesus, was mere semblance without any true reality.

Orthodox iconography, therefore, does not deny the digital image. On the contrary, it will affirm whatever is ontologically significant in digital communications, by opening the digital image to its eternal significance by injecting it with its "future state." With this perspective, the digital image can play an important role in announcing the arrival of eternal ever-being. Consequently, the image can become an "icon" without ceasing to be an image—but only if we who view the image look past the superficial graphic and read the written icon. Maybe it is sufficient for it to be *redeemed* from its association with the past (and the protology of death) while retaining its iconicity. But, we must ask, how may the image be liberated from death and retain its iconicity?

First, we must consider that the *paradox* of the Incarnation was addressed and resolved only in visual-iconic terms. The culture in which we live is subjugated to the representation of reality, either as an evidence-based representation of how things were or are (naturalism) or as a representation with a freedom that distorts the identity of the beings that are represented (modern art). The imminent future will force us to view the world through representations of reality that will become so convincing that our minds could become utterly deceived. "Look at me!"—the claim of the digital image, which renders itself entirely obvious—is a rejection of the *iconic ontology* that automatically results in a different understanding of human existence. Without its referring to the future state, every image is forgotten, becomes the "past," and expires.

Second, an icon bridges the chasm between the three extremes (natural-modern-digital) through the intervention of the person of Christ. Yet, the radical revision of the "virtual" aesthetic can take place in a more comprehensive ecclesial context. Through a bidirectional relation established by the icon, the "object" of what I see suddenly becomes a subject, since it approaches me from outside myself and exerts its influence on me.

Third, the iconic approach presupposes that one accept *a presence to which one can relate*, through an "increasing" perspective. The solution of the *increasing perspective* does not suffer from the fragmentation of information that happens with the optical lens (which at each moment knows only certain sides of an object). For iconic knowledge, there are no front and sides and back.[13]

If the Liturgy is a foretaste of the age to come, then its entire symbolism should point to a transition from a quotidian to an eschatological vision of the world. The Church, thanks most of all to the Liturgy, gives us the certainty that we enter the light and glory of the Resurrection: "Now all things are filled with light."[14] But, if we have an entrance into the Kingdom, that implies a new logic—an *eschatological one*.

Discussions about ecclesial symbolism in our age betray the vagueness of our criteria. Some would like to simplify church symbols (for example, vestments) for ethical (the simplicity of the Gospel) or economic reasons (the money that would've been spent could be given to the poor). These arguments would have weight if the symbolism did not have a deeper meaning.

Orthodox iconography emerged as an attempt to recover the true iconicity of creation and to heal our damaged sensibility by imbuing everything with the ultimate, the "last" (*eschatos*) act of God's will: that "death shall be destroyed."[15] When the storm of iconoclasm broke upon the Church, it denied the premises for salvation: the whole of

[13]Following Stamatis Skliris, I think that the proper term for the Byzantine perspective would be "increasing perspective." I disagree with the term "reverse perspective" used by some because it presupposes an initial "normal" perspective of the Renaissance, which Byzantine art somehow "reverses." Cf. Skliris, *Mirror*, 64.

[14]Pentecostarion, Easter Sunday, Canon Ode 3.

[15]1 Cor 15.26.

divine-human life and liturgical reality, the honor paid to the saints, the matter (ὕλη, *hylē*) which has become filled with divine grace, etc. Therefore, because its *truth*, its raison d'être, was denied, the entire body of the Church reacted, not just intellectuals and learned persons. Truth in genuine art does not simply correspond to the mind or reality. An ecclesial definition of *truth* points to "relationality" and the common ground of existence that we share. This encounter with the divine, in paradox and ambiguity, is a matter of relation rather than logical argumentation. Consequently, an iconographer interprets the event of the resurrected life not in an individualistic way; rather, he or she paints icons with a brush tuned to the vibration of the earthquake that raises the dead and does away with hell. Can we hope that digital images may one day reflect this method and ethos? Our culture so badly needs "information asceticism" and "digital apophatism," by which we mean abstinence from giving the ultimate priority to virtual reality.

Highly conscious of the rich treasure of faith in the holy icons, Christians suitably honor the commemoration of those who bequeathed us this precious heritage, and in so doing rediscover this vision while expecting the ultimate transfiguration of the world that has already begun in the Church. This is the essential meaning of the celebration of the Sunday of Orthodoxy, as it is concisely expressed in the historic *Synodikon* of 843. Regardless of the cost or effort required, the awareness that man is an icon of God must be preserved in our culture.

The Art of Priesthood

(EXCERPTS FROM LETTERS TO A YOUNG PRIEST)

> He's no longer a threat to your monopoly on piety.
> —Pontius Pilate, *Risen*, directed by Kevin Reynolds

"S O JAZZ IS conflict and it's compromise and it's just . . . it's new, *it's brand new every night*. Very, very exciting," says Sebastian Wilder (played by Ryan Gosling) in *La La Land*.[1] To each unpretentious person, who does not commit despicable deeds of egotism—but who is astonished by the mystery of creation—something true is suddenly offered. Because, in the realm of true art, everything is a peaceful surprise.

I begin this letter with a reference to this movie simply because true seekers come to *know* the Church only in the context of *love*, which is an inexhaustible wellspring of surprises. In fact, we enter the Church knowing our brokenness in this world and yearning for newness of life that does not know decay, falseness, and death. With the deepest insights into our insufficiency, a moment of *surprise* comes into our lives unexpectedly, without our contribution. And we discover the Church as a place of the outward experience of true life, a life beyond

---

[1] *La La Land*, directed by Damien Chazelle (Santa Monica, CA: Summit Entertainment, 2016), film.

any natural need. The complete love and humility of the divine-human Lord causes a divine perplexity and surprise that remain forever within you.

Some of us entered the Church because of aesthetics, tradition, duty, or custom, and especially "to socialize." If we stay only because of that, we will miss the point and experience many disappointments. Remember, we do not seek for a distant "God" as a result of our intrinsic need for "religion." In the Church, we have discovered not just "God" but *the One Who Is*, the Loving Person of Christ, the Bridegroom. We all thirst for the unwaning life, but we do not always realize that the possibility of life is available only through a relationship with others in and through the loving God and in *metanoia*, which is to undertake the struggle of repentance.

What do we truly need? What is our real purpose? We do not know. It is revealed to us by somebody else. By the Church. Marveling at this revelation, we then find out the true meaning of the word "church"—a permanent call to a fullness of life. *Ekklēsia* (ἐκ-καλῶ, "to call out"), an invitation to a banquet that never ends, to beauty (τὸ κάλλος). There, in the community of the Church, we learn that "God's will" is the Love of the Father constituted in freedom. Obedience to this love will not let us stray from the mother Church and its beauty.

One day we served the Liturgy in an open space in San Diego County, Southern California. A small stream ran the length of the property, north to south. Mature, native live oaks and other native trees along the stream created a peaceful setting for worship. There were a small number of priests and some thirty faithful who sang at the service. The sun was shining, and the birds were *chirping* persistently from the trees. We reached the central moment of the liturgy, the *anaphora*. When it came time to exclaim, "Singing the victory hymn, proclaiming, crying out . . . ," the priest couldn't resist and suddenly added the word, "*chirping.*" At that moment, as he was chanting, without consciously doing this himself, this sensitivity to God's nature was granted to him, and it surprised him . . . and us.

[. . .] The values embedded within the *art of priesthood* are not moral monuments, sculpted millennia ago, fixed and inert. They are refreshed in each generation by priests who seek to keep their practice in tune with "Christ's mind (γνώμη)"[2] and the prevailing existential needs. A new approach to pastoral art could offer a radical reinterpretation of what one calls "pastoral ministry as a surprise." Just as in the free act of God's creation nonexistence becomes life, so also, in the Resurrection, from the tomb there rises life. Likewise, in the Church, obedience becomes liberty. And this is the gift of surprise.

Look at the many of the most celebrated priests and spiritual fathers—St John of Kronstadt, St Justin Popović, Fr Alexander Schmemann, to name a few. They were seen as radical innovators and risktakers in their own day. The subjects they chose and their insistently new, distinctive approaches transformed pastoral ministry in their times. These priests explored the limits of their ministry, investigating its potential. At the same time, they forged new ways for the faithful to experience the life of the Church. I would say that these avant-garde priests planted the seeds of *renewal* (and not mere "modernism") that would flourish in the third millennium. (Look, for instance, at the style and practice of Serbian Bishop Atanasije: he is the greatest "innovator" and *modernist*, who interprets the dogmas existentially, "translating" them into everyday life; at the same time, he is adamantly *faithful* to the Tradition.)

[2]Cf. Ignatius, *Ephes.* 3.2.

Now, we will admit that the abovementioned exemplary priests are charismatic. Yet, priests who are modest in their abilities but ready to embrace new approaches might still be like them.

[. . .] The "duties" of a priest have an underpinning that is reasonably firm across time. Subtle reworkings of older commitments reveal still further the profound extent of the priest's shifting role. Priests should always put their faithful first, maintain a good standard of pastoral care, show respect, be honest and trustworthy, and keep up-to-date in their knowledge and skills. But the priest in the third millennium might think differently from his earlier counterpart—namely, he might choose to go *against the self-evident*. What do I mean by this?

To illustrate this let me recall an interesting dialogue from the play *Our Town*. When Emily can no longer bear the intensity of what she's seeing, she asks the stage manager, "Do any human beings ever realize life while they live it?—every, every minute?" At first the stage manager answers, "No." But then he adds, "The saints and poets, maybe—they do some."[3] So, perhaps, *only the saints and poets realize life while they live it*. When you accept this new *way* of life and start to live according to it, then, as a priest, you will not be boxed in by human plans. You will articulate yourself in a distinctive semantics.

I like to see among new priests how they explicitly protect and promote both a personal and communal approach to salvation. Nowadays, some want to see the nature of the connection between the faithful and the priest as a personal *partnership*, and not merely a "hierarchical" relationship. But do not have issues with the word "hierarchy"! If a bishop is ready to die for his flock, he is a true hierarch, a servant leader. In the past, leadership was connected to courage. The sister of

[3]Quoted in Stella Adler, *The Art of Acting*, ed. Howard Kissel (New York: Applause Theatre & Cinema Books, 2000), 42.

Blaise Pascal, a nun of Port Royale, when forced to sign something contrary to her faith, noted in the peace of her cell, "As long as bishops act with the courage of girls, then girls must act with the courage of bishops."[4] Leadership (or hierarchy) is indispensable for any faith community. A community deprived of vibrant guidance can be disordered or dispirited. Controlling leadership may create an authoritarian order; yet *participative leadership* can fashion a community that is faithfully animated and dynamic.

You, as the presbyter, are the representative of the bishop in your parish. Since all administration and supervision in the Church stems from the Eucharist, the head of the parish community and council can only be a presbyter, not a layman. You will see that there exists a canonical inconsistency, to be found particularly in the Diaspora, in which a layman is the president of the parish council. I find it to be a symptom of secularization to regard the Church as a democracy in the secular sense and to subject the eucharistic leader to the administrative control of the laity. The laity are an essential part of the Eucharist, without whom there can be no Liturgy. But just as in the Eucharist, so also in the management of the parish (which is nothing but an extension or continuation of the Eucharist in the everyday life of the Church) the laymen are not leaders; they are not shepherds, but the flock. This does not undermine their role, since they remain indispensable, but places them in their proper order. As John Zizioulas says, it is this that makes canon law a matter of dogma and ecclesiology, and not just a matter of administration. Otherwise the administration of the Church will become a secular matter unrelated to the Church. But your ministry must be *charismatically* oriented. If you study the Church, you will

[4]Jacqueline Pascal to Angélique de Saint-Jean Arnauld d'Andilly, June 23, 1661, in Blaise Pascal, *Œuvres complètes*, ed. Jean Mesnard (Paris: Desclée de Brouwer, 1992), 4:1086.

realize that there is nothing in the Church, not even the authority of the bishop or the presbyters, which is not derived from their place in the Eucharist.

[. . .] Certainly, under fire from many quarters, a contemporary priest realizes that his position is not undisputable. In premodern and modern times, a priest could enjoy traditional authority and respect. Yet, when I was younger, somebody told me that I couldn't be a "creator" if I didn't find a way to reconcile in myself the premodern, modern, and postmodern understanding of life. . . . We are all postmodern. We live alongside contemporary people, as if they were the patient in the bed next to us (therefore, by studying man we are studying our own sickness). The basis for this is a respect for one's otherness. The priest should do more to instill in the faithful more courage for responsible action as children of God. And priests will always be held to be personally accountable for their actions.

Study the great fathers, looking for insights and sensitivity. When you studied pastoral theology, you probably created a list of the responsibilities and duties of a priest, but you did not focus on providing a narrative explanation of what it means to be a priest (i.e., a servant leader) in the twenty-first century. Instead, what you learned from documents of exemplary clarity and insight is probably out of touch and even a possible hindrance to emerging new ideas about "pastoral approaches."

The Church becomes not only relevant but revelational in its salvific purpose when we recognize Christ as our Bridegroom. Then everything that is the Church's becomes ours, because we commune with him as with our Beloved One. Love in the Church is a synonym for the ecclesial tasting of resurrected life. When we taste this life then comes an outburst of joy and delight. And we freely and willingly surrender to the Beloved. St Gregory of Nyssa in *Commentary on the Song of Songs* 6 states that the

> end of the bride's advancements becomes a beginning for further
> advancement. . . . But this limit of one's attainment is the begin-
> ning of his/her hope for what lies beyond [and thus we should]
> realize that all perfection of knowledge attainable by human nature
> is only the beginning of a desire for more lofty things.[5]

Everything in the space of the Church that could be superficial,
"learned," mere customary movements, and so forth, can become
transformed, renewed. Censing can become the "fragrancing" of the
bridal chamber of the Coming One; kissing (venerating) an icon can
be "passing to the prototype" a "kiss of peace," a future embrace in God;
hymns turn into an echo of the heavenly, future worship; entrances
become the approach of those who love. "Bless their goings out and
their comings in." "Be exalted like Abraham, O Bridegroom . . . and
you, O Bride, be exalted like Sarah!"[6] Everything acquires being and
comes into existence, so we—spontaneously—cry aloud, "Let every
breath praise the Lord!"

[. . .] As a priest you must not only recognize but also "work within"
the limits of the competence of the faithful. You should "respond to"
faithful preferences, not merely respect those preferences. You will give
the faithful the information they ask for, not only what you think they
want or need. Yet, a priest is not a "service provider." The priest is gifted
with a charisma of the eucharistic transfiguration of the world. In that
way, the faithful will become part of the process of *reshaping* parish
life, rather than only being involved solely in Sunday gatherings. The

---

[5]St Gregory of Nyssa, *Sixth Homily on the Song of Songs* 130; *Gregorii Nysseni Opera* 6, ed. Werner Jaeger (Leiden: Brill, 1986), 180.

[6]Orthodox marriage service, exclamation at the removal of the crowns.

ecclesial ethos is a result of the eucharistic and sacramental manifestations of the Church and of the cooperation between priests and the
faithful. The test is not whether a priest is "fit to practice"—a significant
and burdensome judgment to make about a colleague—but whether
that priest "may be putting the faithful at risk." This introduces the
theme of responsibility toward the faithful. Very often, our relationship with the priesthood operates in closed exchanges of blessing, and
not on a currency of gift.

Your task is to reawaken within your parish a true sense of the
eucharistic offering as something authentic, genuine, and truthful, a
chaste fruit of a community experiencing the Resurrection, the only
true life you want to lead! How about seeing the entire liturgical mysta-
gogy as an iconic representation of the Kingdom? In order to achieve
this iconic ideal, the members of the Church must be attentive to the
true understanding of the liturgical "choreography" and aesthetic
expressions embellishing our worship: beyond any sentimental euphoria, or artificial light effects, and free from didactic expediency and
enthusiastic exhilaration. Our liturgical typicon aims to incorporate
man into a liberated space-time where he can acquire freedom from
all individualistic priorities and become acquainted with the incarnate
Logos, through communion with the Spirit and in personal freedom
and love, beyond the deadly quotidian routine.

This explanation of what good pastoral practice means also signals
a dramatic alteration in the balance between the priest, the faithful,
and the Church. Here, I defend the idea of pastoral *ministry* (not pro-
fessionalism), not only "in action," but also as being a defining set of
ideas that supports the probity of a pastoral practitioner. Indeed, it is
the "goodness" of the priest, and not an abstract and disengaged mani-
festo for good pastoral practice, that should be at the center of your
thinking. Caring about every soul, and staying vigilant in your care of

parishioners. If you are in *modus patiendi* (receptive mode), you will not expect automatic solutions.

[. . .] If you approach the art of priesthood from this viewpoint, you will not be afraid of failing. . . . I will always remember the way Dustin Hoffman, in an *Actors Studio* interview, expressed this important idea:

> Failing is not the worst. Committing a sin is worse. Not failing. Committing a sin. You know, putting something out there that you think is safe and that you think, "Well, I won't get hurt; it's derivative; it's worked before." It's kind of a sin because you're denying yourself your . . . gift, I guess. There's nothing wrong with failing. You're gonna fail. I fail. Everything is, "Success! Success! Success! Success!" Fine! Fine. But give me something that is, "Ooooh!" that's in the, "Oooh!" You know? Let the film not work, let the actor not even be consistent, but put me in there, in that place with somebody. That's worth everything.

The example of the holy Prophet Elijah is quite indicative of this. Endowed with the power and grace of God, he "removes the lightning from the heavens" and hurls it onto the prophets of Baal. He halts the three-year drought, and so forth. Then a woman, Jezebel, banishes him, and, humiliated and powerless, he is forced to hide himself from her for forty days! This is the "mystery of weakness," a so-to-speak "onto-logical" weakness, a crisis that is not simply psychological although profoundly human, through which the greatest saints must go. You must pass through this in full awareness and in all humility, so that you may demonstrate by your own example the truth of salvation, which does not come from oneself (from man) but from the only Holy One.

[. . .] While the partnership and engagement of the faithful are actively encouraged, this is not a green light to drift toward some kind of "anything goes," consumerist ethos in the life of a parish. Effective approaches (and, in some sense, treatments) must be given based on the best available evidence, for instance, Elder Porphyrios's approach.[7] Priests must strive to continuously improve, not merely maintain, their standards of practice. Yes, high standards must repeatedly be reflected in their knowledge and skills, their abilities and competence. Your faithful should feel that they are loved by the community: I am loved, therefore I am! Remember Romans 7.4: "So, my brothers and sisters, you also died to the law through the body of Christ, that you might belong to another (εἰς τὸ γενέσθαι ὑμᾶς ἑτέρῳ), to him who was raised from the dead, in order that we might bear fruit for God." Indeed, "by his resurrection, Christ has finalized the thought that humanity was thinking about for thousands of years without reaching it," says Fr Justin Popović. He adds, "This is the reason St Paul became Christian: his confused soul sought to finalize this great thought without delay—the resurrection as a victory over death."[8]

This experience of surprise will help you to be responsible for protecting the faithful against common, serious, infectious spiritual diseases by ensuring that they are fully immunized with the vaccines of the eucharistic and ascetical ethos. The Church is a place where "love casts out fear."[9] If particular approaches seem harmful, you must report your concerns to your bishop. If those anxieties are ignored, you have a duty to take the matter further. Any action that damages a priest's personal integrity also damages the integrity of the "profession" as a whole.

[7]See *Wounded by Love: The Life and the Wisdom of Elder Porphyrios*, trans. John Raffan (Limni, Evia, Greece: Denise Harvey, 2005).

[8]Justin Popović, *Zapisi, dnevnici, manja dela* [in Serbian] (Belgrade, 2017), 6.

[9]1 Jn 4.18.

[. . .] The priest's vocation is described by St Gregory the Theologian as the "art of arts and the science of sciences" (*Oration* 2.16). So, you must know other arts and sciences. A very wise professor of theology told his students, "For Christ's sake, read some books other than theology!" Before you start a day, it would be good if you prayed. But also, to think of those in need, to visit them.[10] You should speak only about those issues that you have experienced, because, in the Church, nothing is external but *immediate*. Everything we see, hear, or touch together is a disclosure of the incarnated Truth. For example, in the Scriptures, we read, "The life was made manifest, and we saw it" and "that which we have seen and heard," and "that which we have looked upon and touched with our hands" (1 Jn 1.1). So, don't raise any of the essential points of the Gospel unless they awaken you. Remember Elder Porphyrios the New: he was attracted by a power that was relentlessly growing, so he spoke of madness, erotic desire, and intoxication. . . . From then on, the character of our life is changed.

[. . .] You asked about preaching. By "giving word to the Word" (or "honoring the Word with the word," according to St Gregory the Theologian in *Oration* 2.2), a good preacher does not aim to captivate the individual with psychological appeals, but rather to include man in a liberated space-time where he will acquire freedom from all individualistic priorities and become acquainted with the incarnate Logos through communion with the Spirit and in personal freedom and love. In order to reawaken a true sense of the eucharistic offering as something genuine and truthful, the preacher should leave out of his sermon-logos rhetorical excursions into nonecclesial themes. His homilies should truly gather the community and eliminate people's forgetfulness of the eschatological Coming of the Risen One. A homily

[10]Van Gogh first went to serve as a pastor to miners. (Kirk Douglas plays him wonderfully in *Lust for Life*, 1956.)

that does not refer to the Person of Christ is a sermon that refers to the corrupted world. At the end of the day, the listeners are led beyond the word toward the original source of the word, which is a Person.

In this life, we only occasionally realize the truth of authentic life: life means stepping back from the demands of your own life for the sake of the Other's life. The ethos of self-condemnation for the sake of the Other is the fruit of a Christology of *kenōsis*. In an ever more ferocious political and media environment, the integrity and virtue of the profession, as the first lines of defense to protect the faithful's interests, are essential. A priest's personal responsibility and accountability are crucial buttresses supporting trust. Sometimes, love for God invites you to "sacrifice" ethical principles. This is what happens in a story from *The Sayings of the Desert Fathers*. One day Abba Agathon questioned Abba Alonius, saying, "How shall I be willing to restrain my tongue so that it speaks no falsehood?" And Abba Alonius said to him, "Even if you speak no falsehood you are going to commit many sins." "How is that?" said he. The old man said to him, "Here are two men who have committed murder in your sight and one of them has taken refuge in your cell. Then here comes the magistrate, looking for him, and he asks you: 'Was the murder done in your sight?' Unless you speak falsely, you give the man over to death. Better to leave him unshackled in the presence of God, for he knows all."[11]

[. . .] As a priest, you are not merely a skilled observer of human behavior, but the one who is supposed to transmit *life*. Protect and promote the *integral health*, that is, a realistic relationship with God, of other men and the entire creation. Certain tasks and duties seem self-evident. For instance, provide a good standard of practice and confession;

[11]Abba Alonius, Saying 4, in *Give Me a Word: The Alphabetical Sayings of the Desert Fatherts,* trans. John Wortley, Popular Patristics Series 52 (Yonkers, NY: St Vladimir's Seminary Press, 2014), 72.

work with brother priests in ways that best benefit the faithful; treat the faithful as persons politely and considerately and respect their dignity and otherness; respect their right to confidentiality; listen to them, and respond to their concerns and preferences. Act without delay if you have good reason to believe that you or a brother priest may be putting the faithful at risk. Never discriminate unfairly against the faithful or brother priests.

In the Church, we have a blessed assurance, a down payment, incentive, *plērophoria* (Col 2.2; Heb 6.11; Heb 10.22), betrothal, fore-taste. Why is a car's windshield very large and the rearview mirror so small? Maybe because our past is not as important as our future. We should be "forgetting those things which are behind, and reaching forth unto those things which are before."[12]

Most importantly, be prepared, on your own journey to Emmaus, that as soon as you recognize him, he may vanish out of your sight[13] until his next Coming.

[12]Phil 3.13.
[13]Cf. Lk 24.31.

Original Sources of Material

All material previously published is reproduced here with the kind permission of the original publisher(s).

1. "The Beginning and the End Are not the Same (Time in Ecclesial Life)" was first published in Italian in *La eta della vita spiritual, Atti del XXI Convegno ecumenico intenazionale di spiritualita ortodossa, Bose, 4–7 settembre 2013*, a cura di Luigi d'Ayala Valva, Lisa Cremaschi e Adalberto Mainardi monaci di Bose, translated from the original English by Frederico Rigamonti, Edizioni Qiqajon Comunita di Bose 2014, 117–40. It was given as a contribution to the XXI International Conference on Orthodox Spirituality: The Ages of Spiritual Life, organized by the Monastery of Bose, Biella, Italy, September 4–7, 2013.

2. "What Does 'Rising from the Dead' Mean? (Hermeneutics of the Resurrection: The Event of Christ's Resurrection as the Primary Hermeneutical Framework for Each Age)" was given as a contribution to the International Conference on Ontology and History, Delphi, Greece, May 29–31, 2015. Forthcoming.

3. "'We Have Passed Out of Death Into Life' (On the Fear of Death: Theological and Pastoral Reflections)" was first published in *Philotheos* 13 (2013): 84–91. It was given as a presentation at the 2nd International Conference of the Ecumenical Patriarchate for Pastoral Health Care on the theme "Care before the Gates of Death," Rhodes, Greece, October 2011.

4. "How Can We Be Holy and Unique?" appears for the first time in English here.

5. "Does Gender Have a Future? (On Gender and Otherness)" was published in *Philotheos* 11 (2011): 261–69. It was given as a presentation at the International Conference in Honor of the Metropolitan of Pergamon John Zizioulas, Volos, Greece, October 28–30, 2011.

6. "True Freedom as the Conquest of the Self" was published in *Philotheos* 12 (2012): 78–83. It was given as a presentation at the Patriarch Athenagoras Orthodox Institute, hosted by the University of California, Berkeley, May 3, 2011.

7. "'All of Us Are Beggars' (Theological Foundations for an Ecclesial Humanitarianism)" was first published in *Orthodox Christianity and Humanitarianism*, ed. Elizabeth Prodromou and Nathanael Symeonides, special issue of *Review of Faith and International Affairs* 14, no. 1 (Spring 2016): 9–17. It was given as a presentation at the colloquium Orthodox Christianity and Humanitarianism: Ideas and Action in the Contemporary World, Boston, MA, May 7–8, 2015.

8. "Idealizing Politics Abolishes the Eschaton: On Democracy, Human Rights, and Human Dignity," was published in *Philotheos* 17 (2017): 89–96.

9. "Synodality: A Misapprehended Vision," in *Synodality: A Forgotten and Misapprehended Vision*, ed. Maxim Vasiljević and Andrej Jeftić (Los Angeles, CA: Sebastian Press, 2017), 99–124.

10. "Is There Truth in Art?" appears for the first time in English here.

11. "On Digital Iconicity" appears for the first time in English here.

12. "The Art of Priesthood" (from letters to a young priest) is published for the first time here.